Not Going It Alone:

AF207865

Collective Curatorial Curating

Edited by Paul O'Neill
with Gerrie van Noord / Elizabeth Larison

apexart

Praise for *Not Going It Alone: Collective Curatorial Curating*

"Collective practice and collaboration are powerful modes of creation employed first in art, and more recently in the curatorial field. Whether as a means of countering individual authorship or creating the conditions for an individual's voice to resonate in its own context, opening up experimental pathways, or reasserting traditional community values, collective practice is increasingly shaping the cultural landscape. Understanding how is an essential part of making sense of contemporary culture and its global movements. *Not Going It Alone: Collective Curatorial Curating* offers multiple approaches to its subject, making it an important reader for anyone interested in the collective mode of creation, and its many manifestations stemming from the simple act of working together."
— Renaud Proch, Executive & Artistic Director,
Independent Curators International (ICI)

"I believe it's not a matter of erasure of what is called individual as much as it's a matter of assurance against any enclosure of exclusivity or a mob that loses its mind. Collective curatorial practices, as many names addressing and being addressed in this book, unravel a wider vision in which each of us realizes how interdependent and interconnected we are, that's how we make things possible, hence only to acknowledge it without drawing a boundary."
— Binna Choi, curator and Director, Casco Art Institute:
Working for the Commons

"This is a book full of generosity. Collective practices demand a lot of listening and sharing, something that you will find in the many layers of this from now on historical publication."
— Marti Manen, Director, Index – The Swedish
Contemporary Art Foundation

"Exhibitions, events, discussions, and most other manifestations of curatorial work result from collaborative processes. Although only sometimes credited as such, these processes are necessarily collaborative, involving cultural collaborators and administrative, manual, and technical labor, the latter done mainly by uncredited support staff. Who hammers in that nail, arranges the discursive furniture, feeds everyone, empties the trash, and turns off the lights at the end of the day? In what way are those individuals part of the collaboration? *Not Going It Alone* dives into the debate about curating and togetherness and gives hope that such questions will eventually become part of this discussion."
　　— Martin Beck, artist

"Having grown my own curatorial practice through enjoying and admiring many of the curatorial visions analysed in this publication, I feel how timely and necessary, time and again, it is today to assemble, acknowledge, and care for collective intelligence and collaboration of and within the curatorial. The curatorial without the collective effort cannot exist; the curatorial is a collaboration from the beginning phase onwards. This beautifully edited book brings together some of the seminal authors and thinkers, do enjoy it and, if possible, read it in a group."
　　— Nataša Petrešin-Bachelez, interdependent curator,
　　　co-founder of the Initiative for Practices and Visions of
　　　Radical Care

"The entangled crises of our time require collective thinking and creating. With its clear-eyed look at important case studies, this book makes a welcome addition to the curatorial toolbox."
　　— Prem Krishnamurthy, designer, curator, author,
　　　and educator

"Essential reading!"
　　— AA Bronson, artist, co-founder of General Idea

"*Not Going It Alone: Collective Curatorial Curating* offers a sharp critical immersion in the complexities of group creativity and forms of cultural action aimed to de-emphasize individual authorship across different geographies. Rather than reclaiming a single understanding of collective curating, the book pays attention to the potentiality of new forms of togetherness as well as the pitfalls and blind spots associated with unequal distribution of labor. In various ways, the authors seem to ask, 'Who are we speaking of when we say "we"?' Collective infrastructures, participatory processes, and models of co-responsibility appear insistently to remind us of the role of experimentation, trust, openness, and affectivity, as key aspects of (un)learning and expanding what is possible within received forms of curating."
— Miguel A. López, writer and Curator,
Toronto Biennial 2024

"*Not Going It Alone* offers refreshing perspectives on the complex practice of curating with an invaluable collection of case studies of exhibitions and institutions from the 1980s to the present, revealing the rewards—while reminding us of the challenges—of the collaborative nature of the curatorial."
— James Voorhies, Curator, The Bass, and author of
Postsensual Aesthetics: On the Logic of the Curatorial
(MIT Press, 2023)

Publishing © 2024 apexart
Texts © the authors and editors

Printed by:
Printon AS, Tallinn, Estonia

Published by:
apexart, New York.

Visit our website at www.apexart.org.

First printing 2024.

Cataloging-in-Publication data is available
from the Library of Congress.

Design and Cover by Valerio Di Lucente
Initial typesetting by Lisa Vagnoni
Finalized typesetting by Indrek Sirkel

ISBN-13: 978-1-946416-60-5

Contents

INTRODUCTION

*How We Got H*ere:

apexart's Open Call as an expression of collective interests and trends in collective curatorial practices

Elizabeth Larison

It's no secret that exhibitions and related programming presented at established cultural institutions are often determined and curated by relatively closed networks of highly privileged people. While there are some good reasons for this—such as field expertise and experience—it can be also be etremely exclusionary, repetitive, and at times, nepotistic.

Every healthy ecosystem requires diversity. Throughout history, the field of art has thrived on the reimagining of accepted norms and pushing the boundaries of what's familiar through creative experimentation and discovery. In 1994 in New York City, apexart began charting its own attempts at reimagining "business as usual" in the art world, which has introduced an unusual process of group engagement, but has also revealed and supported shifting trends within the field—and in some ways, nearly thirty years later, has led us to the production of this book.

apexart was founded upon principles that emphasized creativity, ingenuity, and—as much as possible—opening up access to those creatives seeking to participate in and contribute to the visual arts. In the following years—a time when curatorial practice was becoming more professionalized, with field-specific graduate programs in their infancy—apexart established itself as an alternative space for independent curators and artists to experiment in ways that were not always feasible within more rigid museum-like exhibition venues. Recognizing that not every would-be curator had access to such professional opportunities, or the connections necessary for entry into the increasingly insular "art world," in 1998 apexart began one of its signature programs: the apexart Open Call.

To this day, the apexart Open Call Exhibition Program accepts text-only exhibition proposals from all over the world that undergo a blind review by a dispersed, international jury. In each Open Call iteration, hundreds of international jurors evaluate and select the winning proposals, which then become apexart exhibitions in New York and beyond. For a cultural institution to relinquish control of its programming selection process—not to a small panel of well-heeled cultural professionals, but to wider audiences regardless of their expertise or affiliation—is highly unusual. As a result, each apexart exhibition season from 1998 onward can be understood as an expression of the curiosities and interests of a broad group of people.

Perhaps because of the unique and experimental nature of this particular opportunity, each Open Call attracts hundreds of proposals that are a strong reflection of what is happening in the art world, and that reflect the current cultural moment more generally.

Invariably, each pool of submissions has its trending topics that reflect urgent issues arising in the arts and in society at large, from the hyperlocal to the global: issues pertaining to human migration, geopolitics, ecological crises, racial inequality, corrective alternative histories, gender and sexual identity, and so on. In the years that I worked at apexart, and before, there was also another kind of trend that reached beyond the typical ebb and flow of interests: we observed a shift in how the proposals themselves were shaped, and who was shaping them.

Reflecting upon wider movements in the art world, apexart saw an increase in proposals coming from people working collaboratively in a myriad of ways. We saw artists coming together for the first time to pitch a show of their own work based on a singular theme; established arts collectives proposing projects that built upon the individual, stand-alone works of their members; one-off curatorial collaborations in which two or more curators would join together for the singular proposed project; established curatorial collectives who intentionally and decisively work with one another across multiple exhibitions and other cultural projects; and activist-minded groups or researchers from non-arts fields seeking to communicate their ideas into an experimental and arts-driven format—the collaborative relations seemed to come in all imaginable forms.

Whatever the case, there appeared to be an implicit interest in working together as part of a curatorial approach that was demonstrated among those submitting exhibition proposals to apexart: whether as a matter of principle, logistical facility via delegation and skill sharing, of purpose, or of something else all together.

We also saw distinct trends that focused on reimagining project formats and audience engagement. The apexart Open Call model requires winning curators or curator-groups to develop companion programming, and proposals routinely appear to focus on ever-expanding methods of audience-engagement efforts to interact with and activate their intended viewership. Proposals to apexart's opportunity, and those submitting them, typically address specific social and cultural issues, which reveal an increased focus on aspects such as community engagement, education opportunities, and activism. Every year, apexart sees a substantial fraction of proposals seeking to facilitate interactivity and participation. These efforts can be understood as complicating the default model of "art for looking at"—and not much else—in a space.

In a way, the apexart Open Call could be seen as not just a reflection of collective interests of dispersed groups, but as a "real time" indicator of trends in collaborative curatorial practices. While institutional curatorial practice and scholarship in the last 25 years has been making a marked, but cumbersome effort to develop and integrate models of inclusivity, and respond to and incorporate collective approaches to art making and curatorial practice, apexart's Open Call model has fostered these developments by simply giving away the reins in its selection process and providing opportunities for different kinds of collaborations to take place... and succeed. It was from these reflections, and outcomes, that the idea for this book originated.

With the guidance and vision of Paul O'Neill, we've been able to expand the scope of this book beyond self-reported reasons for and processes of collective curatorial work, and move toward a more nuanced understanding: its relevance in art history, in varying contemporary geopolitical contexts and applications, and as an extension of humans existing among and learning with one another. Here we look at collaborative work as it pertains to curating exhibitions, but also at a kind of group-mindedness through the approaches and processes of the curatorial—whether it involves co-creation, co-research, or community engagement through programming or audience activation and consideration. Because, importantly—and as noted in the variety of relations that aspiring apexart co-curators shared with one another—there is no one way to collaborate, or think collaboratively. Here, we examine this diversity in an effort to better understand what its possibilities and limitations might entail, and what might be its impact upon the field as a whole.

Notably, group-driven curatorial processes often entail an emphasis on process over specific outcome, a focus on inclusion and accessibility, and a departure from well-trodden, tried and tested methods—a kind of openness and sometimes unruliness, not unlike the process of the Open Call that led (some of) us here in the first place.

The resulting collection of essays is by no means an exhaustive overview of collective, collaborative, or group curating, nor of the many ways in which such practices have expanded to date. However, its contents are incredibly generous in how they open up critical spaces that both enhance and reflect a nuanced understanding of curatorial collaboration.

*C*ollaboration

Nikolett Erőss / Eszter Lázár

Collaboration is the generic name for dialogical activities which bring about artworks, exhibitions, or projects.[1] Pre-eminently, these are situations in which a group of people—rather than an individual artist, curator, or participant—work and develop a concept together. Instead of following the long tradition of object-centered artistic production, these practices favor *process*—dialogue among diverse communities (→*discursivity,* →*performativity*). Collaborative practices often expand the terrain of contemporary art, in order to involve social, economic, or political issues (→*curatorial,* →*interpretation*).

Depending on the combination of participants and the relationship between them, different but synonymous terms have evolved to name these processes, including cooperation, interaction, collective action, or participatory practices. Collaboration can take place between artists (artists' groups) and curators (collective curating); various partners active outside the art scene can also be involved. Collaboration is an open-ended concept, encompassing several approaches. In the case of cooperation (based on the notion of collaboration), this is of mutual benefit to the partners. However, with participation, members can only shape the unfolding of a situation, the framework of which has been predefined by someone else.[2] The realm of collaboration can also be extended with new terms—such as dialogical art, conversational art, littoral art, and new genre public art—in which, in addition to the dialogical relationship between artists and their partners, the dialogue becomes a part of the "work" itself.

The participants (artists, curators, actors from the social field) in contemporary collaborative art practices have an important position in mediating new social meanings through their shared responsibility as not only content but also context providers (→ curatorial).[3] One of the most important aspects of all collaborations in art is that social criticism and social impact are mediated through art. Self-organization, as a form of collaboration, is itself a productive and empowering strategy, which could lead to broader cultural and social impact, linking new forms of inter-subjective experiences with political activism.[4]

Collaboration carries with it important implications for the role of the viewer. Once a passive figure confined to visual perception, minimalism, installation art, and other spatial practices, especially performance art, have reinvested the viewer with their bodily sensation, and physical activity has become vital to experiencing the artwork. This entails the emancipation of the viewer and the revision of traditional power relations defining artist-institution-viewer dynamics. Furthermore, while art was shifting from the practice of producing objects, movements like conceptualism, happenings, and Fluxus—informed by a wide range of performative practices— decoupled participation from physicality. These art practices therefore started to involve the audience in performing collective art-making, bringing art closer to everyday life and experience. Rather than accentuating the authorial position of the individual, those genres most appropriate to collective authorship were foregrounded by artists' groups in the 1960s. This can be examined as an antecedent to contemporary collaborative practices, in which joint initiatives—combining political engagement and activist endeavors—can be linked, first and foremost, to alternative forms of knowledge production.[5] Moreover, collaboration can also be considered within the trajectory of site-specific art practices since the 1960s, in which the remit of the site was expanded to include the public, and, later, the community (→*interpretation*).[6]

Collaboration is also an important aspect of work between curators. In the case of collective curating—a growing tendency in the curatorial practice of recent decades—the curatorial vision is formed by multiple voices, rather than an individual (authorial) voice, and shared decision-making is accentuated during the realization of the project. Collective curatorial methods are not only characterized by marginal initiations but are also significantly affected by the globalized biennial network, which is often manifested in the appropriation of (once) alternative methods.

The critical literature on collaboration takes up issues related to structure, working methods, and motivation; the question of authorship (the responsibility of authors), the aesthetic and ethical parameters of collaborative processes, and the outcome of projects. Among the writers and critics developing the theoretical foundation of such practices, Grant Kester and Claire Bishop represent a definitive, if fruitful, opposition. While valorizing events and projects with the potential for social disruption, Bishop argues in favor of the autonomy of artists and the aesthetic criteria of their works, which, in certain cases, might predominate over equality. By contrast, Kester argues for consensual collaboration, offering solutions to particular sociopolitical problems instead of cultivating the artist's privileged position. Such critical approaches toward relational art (→*performativity*) have also contributed to debates around dialogical, community-based art forms. Relational art requires participation, but its formalism is much criticized, as the choreography of the work is principally predesigned by the artist, delimiting the subjective encounters that the works intend to establish within a hermetic, institutionally framed environment.

In the past few years, collaborative groups—comprised of flexible memberships and short-term projects—carved out new possibilities which could contribute to their effectiveness, thanks to global communication networks and the mobility of privileged actors. The increased mobility of otherwise institutionally empowered artists may, however, run the risk of producing superficial encounters with members of certain communities, which restrict shared interest and mutual understanding. Although collaborative practices characterize most of the socially engaged and activist art projects that involve various communities and individuals (→ *discursivity*), they are increasingly criticized for instrumentalizing collaboration to gain political legitimization, justifying the artist's intention or the public funding invested in the project.

1   Collaboration and collaborator held negative connotations in Europe after World War II. They were used to refer to those who, during the French Vichy regime and occupation of other countries, cooperated with the Germans. Today, however, the word collaboration is often used as a synonym for "working together."

2   Maria Lind, "The Collaborative Turn," in *Taking the Matter into Common Hands: On Contemporary Art and Collaborative Practices*, ed. Johanna Billing, Maria Lind, and Lars Nilsson (London: Black Dog Publishing, 2007), 15–31.

3   Grant Kester, *Conversation Pieces: Community and Communication in* *Modern Art* (Berkeley: University of California Press, 2004).

4   See also Stine Herbert and Anne Szefer Karlsen, eds., *Self-organised* (London/Bergen: Open Editions/ Hordaland Art Centre, 2013).

5   Lind, "The Collaborative Turn."

6   See also Hal Foster, "The Artist as Ethnographer," in *The Return of the Real* (Cambridge, MA: MIT Press, 1996), 302–09; and Miwon Kwon, *One Place after Another: Site-Specific Art and Locational Identity* (Cambridge, MA: MIT Press. 2002); as well as Paul O'Neill and Claire Doherty, eds., *Locating the Producers: Durational Approaches to Public Art* (Amsterdam: Valiz, 2011).

This is a slightly edited version (in terms of spelling and punctuation) of Eszter Lázár and Nikolett Erőss, "Collaboration" as part of tranzit.hu, "Curatorial Dictionary: Unpacking the Oxymoron," in Curatorial Research, ed. Paul O'Neill and Mick Wilson (London: Open Editions, 2014). The original version was written in 2012 by Eszter Lázár, for Curatorial Dictionary, ed. Eszter Szakács, available at https://tranzit.org/ curatorialdictionary/index.php/dictionary/collaboration/ (accessed March 20, 2023).

Beyond Trending:

Group Practices in Art and Curating

Paul O'Neill

Artists' Groups and Group-Exhibitions as Form

"SHUT THE FUCK UP!" shout General Idea in their mockumentary
with the same title from 1985. Looking directly into the camera, three
young artists—AA Bronson, Felix Partz, and Jorge Zontal—continue
their rant:

> I am not going to be a media whore, I won't play bad guy
> to your good guy, boohoo to your bourgeoisie, we are
> supposed to be romantic, untamed, while our artworks are
> slipped back into the marketplace, blue-chip investments
> for level-headed fetishists […] I'd like to paint them into
> a corner, I am not going to shit on a canvas and they'll call it
> art, it doesn't matter what they are saying as long as they
> are talking […] no matter what they will dress you up […] do
> you get the picture, do you know what to say, SHUT THE
> FUCK UP!

General Idea's high-camp critique of the art world and the mass media and their clichéd image of the solitary artist offered a then timely reminder of how both populist media and contemporary art discourses often translate the complexities of any group practice into quantifiable products and marketable identities. In their attempts to undermine their mediation within the art world, General Idea highlighted the art world's capacity to maintain its investment in a falsified image of the creative individual, despite such critiques. General Idea's enduring relevance serves as an indicator of how little has changed since the early 1980s in relation to the institution of the individual producer. In times of increased preoccupations with care, togetherness, and collectiveness, it is worth asking (again, or rather still) if the merging of people and practices really offers any sustainable resistance to the cult of creative individualism, or whether "collective" is just another marketable brand in disguise.

When I interviewed Bronson in 2005, he explained that General Idea was modeled on the idea of a rock band, saying "We thought of ourselves in really pragmatic terms as a group. I think if any of us had played instruments, we would have formed a proper rock band. We didn't think of ourselves as a collective."[1] Bronson highlighted a distinction between the liberating potentiality of a "group," formed out of mutual friendship, and a "collective," understood as a restrictive structure guided by a dominant ideological or organizational principle. Artists' groups such as General Idea were central to underlining that exhibitions are always "group" formations already—in as much as they speak on behalf of the group about *how* art is seen as much as about *which* art is seen—and that artists who consider the spaces in which their work is displayed as part of their strategic remit can be argued to effectively "curate" their own extended practice. General Idea's multifarious approaches to mediation, distribution, and collaboration—which included publishing other artists' projects alongside their own in their self-published *FILE Megazine* (1972–89), and the establishment of Art Metropole as a distribution center and exhibition space for artists' editions and multiples—moved the parameters of group curatorial work beyond the gallery space into multiple channels of dissemination.

With its rotating cast of members between 1979 and 1996, Group Material also used the process of exhibition-making as a space for political and social formation, where the exhibition functioned as a shared site of participation among individuals, and the event of the exhibition enabled a social public forum and a place for discussion. Exhibitions such as *The People's Choice* (1981) challenged the standardized manners in which art had come to be displayed and how such conventions were established. Interrupting the traditional museum collection model, *The People's Choice* presented material selected by non-professional cultural experts and local residents were invited to contribute objects from their homes to the exhibition on East 13th Street in New York City. *Americana*, shown in the context of their first institutional presence at the 1986 Whitney Biennial, comprised a *salon des refusés* of marginalized artists with socio-political concerns alongside products from supermarkets and department stores, breaking the boundaries between high and low culture by questioning the function of cultural representation and hierarchies of cultural production. Their subsequent *Democracy* (1987–89) show at the DIA Foundation was organized as a cycle of discussion-led events and collaborative shows divided into four sections: "Education and Democracy," "Politics and Election," "Cultural Participation and AIDS," and "Democracy: A Case Study."[2] All these projects examined the complexities of classification and conventional modes of presentation, while stressing the need for more transdisciplinary and discursive approaches to curating, beyond the confines of the conventional exhibition as form. They underlined that all group exhibitions, whatever form they take, are the result of divergent, complex, and dialectical relations—between curators, artists, and all others provided with some form of agency in the process of production. By making these interrelations apparent from the outset, and in articulating the means of production, "the difference[s] between collaborative and authorial structures,"[3] converged during a process of co-production, leading to the construction of co-operative and co-authored group exhibitions.[4]

Collective, Collaborative Turns

The interest in collaboration in the first decade of this century saw an increase in self-organized initiatives, accompanied by survey exhibitions, publications, and projects that brought these organizational networks together under a single rubric. This raised the question whether any collective art project or group work had the potential to still be subsumed by a single author in the same way as a self-contained artwork. When General Idea declared that working in a group had freed them from the tyranny of individual genius; when Art & Language (A&L) attempted to embody an aesthetic practice that escaped from "prevailing stereotypes of artistic personality" and the figure of the romanticized individual artist by becoming a changing group of artists making art, using ideas, words, and textual forms, turning away from the artist-as-maker and toward art-as-a-language even in its name, A&L[5]; or when Group Material made a plea for an understanding of creativity as unrestricted by the marketplace or by categories of specialization, they all expressed a common desire for an alternative to the autonomous figure of the artist, as much as the curator and the critic. The significance of Group Material and General Idea as precedents for an increasing turn to group work was highlighted when they were selected as part of the exhibition *Collective Creativity* at Kunsthalle Fridericianum in Kassel in 2005. This major exhibition, and the supporting publication, posited the view that all creative work was always collaborative in principle, if not in name, while explicitly articulating group work as some form of resistance to the dominant, market-driven model of production supported by existing socio-cultural institutions.

The curators of the show, the Zagreb-based curatorial collective WHW (What, How & for Whom) have not been the only ones calling for greater visibility of group practices over the years, with collective work presented as the results of alternative forms of sociability—even if their objectives fail to have any lasting effect beyond the social subsystem that is the art world. Their *Collective Creativity* documented historical avant-garde models such as Dada, Surrealism, and Fluxus, alongside an eclectic mix of contemporary group activities from (former) Western and Eastern Europe, Latin America, and the United States. As such, the project reflected upon a wide variety of heterogeneous approaches to multiple authorship across social, cultural, and historical divides. WHW presented the project as an act of kinship, a show of solidarity with the general spirit of collectivism shared by many of the assembled exhibitors, for whom joint work provided a utopian cooperative space for critical discourse.

In their introductory essay for the catalogue, WHW declared that *collective creativity* calls upon the emancipatory potential of communist(ic) forms of work and collaborative production for the good of the whole, through which individual energies are bundled together and common interests prevail, or a shared result is achieved.[6] Herein lay, however, also one of its problems. The packaging of all these groups as a common "collective" translated into a flattening of the specificity of group formation, where Group Material became interchangeable with General Idea with Gilbert & George with IRWIN. The reason for this is that it was hard to avoid perceiving "collective creativity" as representing a benevolent, idealistic, notion of *all* collective work. What was common to each of these groups is that individuals within them preferred to work with specific rather than generic others. As much as the show demonstrated how all work is collaborative, each initiative had distinct cultural formations and capacities for action, depending on their access to and/or engagement with their means of production. This raised the question of why there seemed to continue to be a need to conceive of "collectivity" as a single unified "creative" body, as a binary construct at the other end of the spectrum of "individual." WHW offered a similar observation as self-critique when they stated,

> We are not primarily interested in exploring the formal structure of organizations (networks, communities, groups, platforms, etc.), as much as their attempts to redefine the categories of site, status and the function of art in the public space. Although there are many common sites of departure, organized networks and self-organized practices are not a unified movement.[7]

Such assessment was notable throughout their ambitious Istanbul Biennial of 2009, titled *What Keeps Mankind Alive*, in which they portrayed an allied but non-unified global art multitude, while being explicit about the specific demographics of their selection. They demonstrated how extensive group research is part of any curatorial process, which like art, is often curtailed by lack of access to the means of production.[8] Extending their ongoing approach, WHW successfully breached the institutional walls of Kunsthalle Wien in 2019 when three of its members, Ivet Ćurlin, Nataša Ilić, and Sabina

Sabolović, were jointly appointed as its directors following the departure of Nicolaus Schafhausen.[9]

What is crucial to underline at this point is that models of collaboration have increasingly been associated with contextual and dialogical procedures rather than material outcomes, and led to new terms of engagement in social networking projects. Classifying labels such as "conversational art" (Homi K. Bhabha), "dialogical art" (Grant Kester), "new genre public art" (Suzanne Lacy), "new situationism" (Claire Doherty), "connective aesthetics" (Suzi Gablik), "participatory art" (Claire Bishop), "social practice art" (Gregory Sholette), "Arte Útil" (Tania Bruguera), or "curatorial activism" (Maura Reilly) have all attempted to encapsulate the discursive qualities of "publicness" inherent in more immaterial forms of collective artistic co-production that is predominantly experienced beyond the institutional setting or the gallery frame. All these terms have attempted to grasp how multiple participants in art are involved as co-creators, with a view to shaping public spaces.[10] In these cases, the function of the artwork is to create situations in which whoever is part of the group can potentially have agency in the processes initiated by the artist. The artwork is put forward as the accumulation of interactions and configured as a cluster of participant-driven social- and community-responsive interventions gathered over time, which eventually result in some kind of public manifestation. The result is group work conceived as a processual curatorial endeavor as much as post-autonomous artistic practice.

Curatorial Turning Collective as Institutional Forms

Meanwhile, interdisciplinary discussions, talks, conferences, and educational programs have become integral parts of exhibitions and art fairs alike, accommodating the participation of less materialized and more discursive modes of group practice. Historically, these discursive program elements were peripheral to the exhibition, operating in a secondary role in relation to the display of art for public consumption. In the last two-to-three decades, these discursive interventions and relays have become central to contemporary practice, and in some cases are the main event or "exhibition."[11] Early iterations have been categorized as being part of the so-called "educational turn," prompted by the recurrent mobilization of pedagogical models within curatorial strategies and critical art projects.[12] Such hybrid art projects often manifested this engagement with educational and pedagogical formats and motifs diverging in terms of scale, purpose, *modus operandi*, value, visibility, reputation, and degree of actualization. However, even a cursory glance at the many modes, twists, and turns of education, its modalities and forms, highlights the propensity of work that foregrounded collective action and collaborative discursive praxis.[13] These initiatives questioned how we might restructure, re-think, and reform the way in which we speak to one another in a group setting. Without over-simplifying these projects, they can generally be described as a critique of formal educational processes and the way these processes form subjects.

Attempts to historicize collaborative practices include widely cited publications such as the trend setting anthology *Self-Organization/ Counter-Economic Strategies* (2006), edited by Will Bradley, SUPERFLEX et al., or Claire Bishop's much cited anthology on *Participation* (2006), as well as other edited gatherings such as *Taking the Matter into Common Hands* (2007) and Bishop's *Artificial Hells: Participatory Art and the Politics of Spectatorship* (2012). Together these function as toolboxes for self-organized activities as well as reflections upon the theoretical formulations of the many kinds of participation and collaboration in art and curating.[14] The proliferation of the wide range of projects described reveals how ubiquitous certain collective and self-organized models have become. With all this togetherness going on, it is worth considering distinctions between self-enterprises in disguise, which function as a self-help conduit to the curatorial market, and co-productive models that use social processes of communication based on a shared language.

When a new generation of curators emerging in the 1990s began to show an interest in co-operative, process-orientated, discussion-based mode of exhibitions, they worked closely with artists and one another. These collaborations happened on the premise that concealing the curator's role as something akin to a neutral provider only reinforced the modernist myth that artists work alone, their practice unaffected by those they work with. As a result, artistic and curatorial practice converged in a variety of projects seeking to undermine the idea that the production, reception, and interpretation of art could ever occur without the advice, suggestions, and interventions of "procreative" curators, critics, and production partners. This led to the emergence of curatorial practice as a central focus and paradigm for experimentation, for new formats of collective cultural action, and greater emphasis on self-organization. The ascendant discourse of curating can be argued to have intensified discursivity in approaches to exhibition production, with curators tending to work closely with artists on the overall schema or on longer co-productions.[15]

And although discussions and debates on exhibitions have continued to mobilize an expanded, centralized position for the figure of the curator, there has been a punctuated shift away from the "single author," gradually moving toward more collaborative, discursive and collective models of curating. To be able to sustain an inclusive model of production, like artists, curators have increasingly taken on collective models that manifest the merits of group work. Even a brief glance at developments of large-scale international events reveals how group curating has become a mainstay on the biennial circuit, for either pragmatic or ideological reasons. Curatorial groups—from WHW to Raqs Media Collective to ruangrupa—as well as established global curators-turned-institutional directors—from Charles Esche to Maria Lind, Okwui Enwezor, and Ute Meta Bauer—have maintained a common argument for collaborative curatorial models throughout their practice, particularly when such exhibitions demand access to a wider network of artistic and cultural practices. Whether working as part of an enforced team (Manifesta, since 1996), or selected by the artistic director to work on the overall concept (Okwui Enwezor's documenta11, 2002), or as a bunch of semi-autonomous curators overseen by an artistic director (Francesco Bonami's 50th Venice Biennale, 2003), co-curating has developed into a dominant working model for most perennial shows, including the last versions of Istanbul, Tirana, São Paulo, and Berlin.[16] While the discourse around collaboration and collectivity has focused largely on examples from the West/Global North, in recent years attention has embraced examples of collaborative and group practices from the Global South, not least enhanced by documenta 15's "collective of collectives."

Although not without their problems, group work has demonstrated the advantages of pooling knowledge resources, networks, and opinions, as well as prefacing them with a symbolic critique of the cult of individualism. However, this increase in "togetherness" has not meant the end of curator-led authorship, with continued precedence in 2007 with Roger Buergel and Ruth Noack's documenta 12 and Robert Storr's Venice Biennale, the latter followed by single-author visions in iterations curated by Daniel Birnbaum, Bice Curiger, Massimiliano Gioni, Enwezor, Christine Macel, Ralph Rugoff, and most recently Cecilia Alemani, and the recently appointed first Latinx curator Adriano Pedrosa, respectively. The same happened in Istanbul, with Hou Hanru, Carolyn Christov-Bakargiev, Fulya Erdemci, and Nicolas Bourriaud taking the lead one after the other, with artist duo Elmgreen and Dragset among the odd blips in 2017. The 2021 iteration picked up the baton of group work again, although it was a collaborative rather than collective endeavor, this time between Ute Meta Bauer, Amar Kanwar, and David Teh.

Other significant, yet diverse projects in most recent times—such as Eastside Projects in Birmingham, Casco and BAK in Utrecht, Index in Stockholm, BétonSalon or La Colonie in Paris, HomeWorks in Beirut, SAVVY in Berlin, Raw Material Company in Dakar, The Indigenous Curatorial Collective in Toronto, Gudskul in Jakarta, Chimurenga in Cape Town, or the nomadic If I Can't Dance…—have reimagined the group exhibition format by taking on performative and accumulative approaches, in which public exhibition programs evolve in parallel with the evolution, or even formation, of their organization/institution.[17] These include curatorial projects stretching out over time, working things out through doing, making things appear by performing them, employing the exhibition moment as a research tool for further investigation—and thus configuring curatorial practice as part of an evolving, episodic, discursive, and perpetually unfolding collaborative network.

As curatorial work has become more collaborative, exhibitions now also include non-specialist art practitioners and involve participation across various cultural fields of inquiry. In more recent curatorial projects, the triangular network of artist, curator, and audience has been replaced by a spectrum of potential inter-relationships, which has led to the notion of "the curatorial"—note the quotation marks—as identified and espoused by Jean-Paul Martinon, Irit Rogoff, Maria Lind, Beatrice von Bismarck, and others, including myself.[18] Such a shift in the understanding of authorship,

as something beyond the mind and hand of an individual,
acknowledges the idea that art is neither produced in isolation nor
should it be understood as being autonomous from the rest of life.
As curator Charles Esche stated already in the late 1990s:
"We are all collaborators in the pursuit of the art experience as
a transformative, hopefully life-enhancing thing."[19]
When Hans Ulrich Obrist quipped that "collaboration is the
answer, but what is the question?" some two decades ago, he was
probably alluding to the necessary function of such questions for
sustaining his essentially eternal interviews projects. He may equally
have been thinking about how collaborative practice is so often
reduced to an individual statement and deemed to be on behalf of
someone, but he did observe the start of what would become a sea
change of sorts from collaboration to collective practices.[20] Already
in 2010, this tendency was taking on divergent models of group
work, such as Manifesta 8 being organized by three interdisciplinary
collectives (Alexandria Contemporary Arts Forum, Chamber of Public
Secrets, and tranzit.org); the 2019 Lyon Biennale being curated by
an institutional team (Palais de Tokyo); and the Berlin Biennale 11
in 2020 led by a "four-voice constellation" of María Berríos, Renata
Cervetto, Lisette Lagnado, and Agustín Pérez Rubio. By the
2020s this trend has extended to significant institutional support. In
2021, the shortlist for the UK's Turner Prize comprised five artist-
curator collectives—Array Collective, Black Obsidian Sound System
(B:O:S:S), Cooking Sections, Gentle/Radical, and Project Art
Works. For the documenta 15 iteration in 2022, ruangrupa invited
other collectives, and groups such as OFF-Biennale, NEST
Collective, Trampoline House, and Wajukuu Art Project, among many
other self-organized and para-institutions being brought into
their curatorial remit as part of what they call an "ecosystem" for
collaborative projects.[21]

　　Returning to where I started, with General Idea, it may be
possible to shed some light on the reason for this ongoing and
expanding interest in working with others. *Felix, June 5, 1994* (1995),
a large public billboard depicting a scaled-up image of Felix Partz
laid out in his bed, eyes wide open, his skeletal face looking down
from high up above, was General Idea's final collaborative work.
Felix is surrounded by his most beloved possessions: wrapped
in multi-colored bedclothes, his head is resting upon a bright yellow

pillow. He is wearing his favorite shirt, buttoned all the way up, covering his body, emaciated by the illnesses that brought about his demise. It is a beautiful, yet unsentimental picture of death. As a deeply moving image of a lost friend, taken by AA Bronson, it reminds us that the foundation of any group creativity is the common bond of friendship. *Felix, June 5th, 1994* acts as an emotive signifier for all group work. It tells us that all groups are made up of individuals who happen to believe in art, who like working together, and who sometimes even love each other. Maybe, unintentionally, or perhaps unwittingly, it also shows us how much so many of us would rather not go it alone.

1   Paul O'Neill in conversation with AA Bronson, New York, May 28, 2004, edited by Bronson June 4, 2006.

2   For more on Group Material's practice, see Julie Ault, "Thee Snapshots from the Eighties: On Group Material," in *Curating Subjects*, ed. Paul O'Neill (London: Open editions, 2007); Julie Ault, ed., *Show and Tell: A Chronicle of Group Material* (London: Four Corner Books, 2010); and Julie Ault, "Active Recollection: Archiving 'Group Material,'" in *Self-Organised*, ed. Stine Hebert and Anne Szefer Karlsen (London/Bergen: Open Editions/ Hordaland Art Centre, 2013), 102–12.

3   In his keynote address for the Banff 2000 International Curatorial Summit at the Banff Centre on August 24, 2000, Bruce Ferguson highlighted three recurring issues in contemporary curating, the third of which was "the difference between collaborative and authorial structures." See Melanie Townsend, "The Troubles with Curating" in *Beyond the Box: Diverging Curatorial Practices*, ed. Melanie Townsend (Banff: Banff Centre Press, 2003), xv.

4   There have, over time, of course been many groups and collectives that through working with others challenged systemic conventions and

traditions, such as the Independent Group, Godzilla, Gutai, or Colectivo Acciones de Arte, to name but a few. My aim here is not to provide an overview as such, but to consider the effects of group practices.

5   As Charles Harrison states in Charles Harrison, *Essays on Art & Language* (Oxford/ and Cambridge, MA: Basil Blackwell, 1991), 91–92.

6   See WHW, "New Outlines of the Possible," in *Collective Creativity*, ed. René Block and Angelika Nollert (Frankfurt: Revolver, 2005).

7   Cited from an interview with WHW in a press release for *What is an Organisation?*, October 25, 2008, Spike Island, Bristol, organized by Paul O'Neill and Situations. See also What How and for Whom (WHW), *What Keeps Mankind Alive? Guide to the 11th Istanbul Biennial* (Istanbul: Istanbul Foundation for Culture and Arts, 2009).

8   In the catalog essay, for instance, they stated that 28% of the artists selected were born in Europe and North America, but 45% were now residing there. Of the 70 artists represented, 22 were living outside of their country of origin (27 artists originally being from the Middle East, 18 from Eastern Europe, 10 from Western Europe, 5 from Central

Asia, and so on). With less than half of the artists residing in the West, 38 different nationalities were represented, providing an indication of the diasporic nature of the art world via a curatorial statement. See WHW, *What Keeps Mankind Alive?*, 22–27.

9   Less than a year later, the global Covid-19 crisis struck, and, like their compatriots at arts institutions around the world, WHW were faced with tremendous economic and logistical challenges in running the institution. Effective June 2024, they have been ousted from their leadership role at Kunsthalle Wien. According to Austrian daily *Der Standard*, the city government issued an open call for applicants for the role of director at the institution, but all twenty, including WHW, were found wanting by a six-person panel, and at the time of writing a new director has yet to be appointed. See https://www. artforum.com/news/curatorial-collective-whw-ousted-from-kunsthalle-wien-leadership-89858 (accessed March 20, 2023).

10 As seen in some of the people-based artist projects by Bruguera, Can Altay, Temporary Services, Oda Projesi, Ultra Red, Skart, Kathrin Böhm, Park Fiction, Rick Lowe, Blank Noise, Ahmet Öğüt, Apolonija Šušteršič, or Jeanne van Heeswijk. See Claire Bishop, "The Social Turn: Collaborations and its Discontents," *Artforum,* February 2006, 178–83; and Maria Lind, "Complications: On Collaboration, Agency and Contemporary Art," *Public, Art, Culture, Ideas*, no. 39, "New Communities," spring 2009, 52–73. Other early publications of significance on collective social practices of note include Gregory Sholette and Blake Stimson, *Collectivism After Modernism: The Art of Social Imagination after*

1945 (Minneapolis: University of Minnesota, 2007); and Gregory Sholette and Nato Thompson, *The Interventionists: A User Manual for the Creative Disruption of Everyday Life* (North Adams, MA: Mass MOCA, 2006).

11 See Paul O'Neill and Mick Wilson, eds., *Curating and the Educational Turn* (Amsterdam/London: De Appel/ Open Editions, 2010); and Mick Wilson, "Curatorial Moments and Discursive Turns," in Paul O'Neill, ed., *Curating Subjects* (Amsterdam/ London: de Appel/Open Editions, 2007).

12 Ibid.

13 Kristina Lee Podesva proposed that "education as a form of art making constitutes a relatively new medium. It is distinct from projects that take education and its institution, the academy, as a subject or facilitator of production." Drawing on research by the Copenhagen Free University and others, Podesva itemizes ten characteristics and concerns across a spectrum of education-as-medium projects. These include: "A school structure that operates as a social medium"; "A tendency toward process (versus object) based production"; "An aleatory or open nature"; "A post-hierarchical learning environment where there are no teachers, just co-participants"; "A preference for exploratory, experimental, and multi-disciplinary approaches to knowledge production"; "An awareness of the instrumentalization of the academy." See Kristina Lee Podesva, "A Pedagogical Turn: Brief Notes on Education as Art," *Fillip*, no. 6. 2007, available at http://fillip.ca/ content/a-pedagogical-turn (accessed March 16, 2023). It is also worth looking at Anton Vidokle's "Incomplete Chronology of Experimental Art Schools," in *Notes for an Art School*

(Amsterdam: International Foundation Manifesta, 2006), 19.

14 See Claire Bishop, *Participation* (London/Cambridge, MA: Whitechapel Gallery/MIT Press, 2006); Maria Lind, Johanna Billing, and Lars Nilsson, *Taking the Matter into Common Hands* (London: Black Dog Publishing, 2007); Will Bradley, SUPERFLEX, Mika Hannula, and Cristina Ricupero, eds., *Self-Organization/Counter-Economic Strategies* (Sternberg Press, 2006); and Bishop, *Artificial Hells: Participatory Art and the Politics of Spectatorship* (Verso, London, 2012).

15 For example, when Maria Lind curated *What If? Art on the Verge of Architecture and Design*, at the Moderna Museet in Stockholm in 2000, she invited artist Liam Gillick to participate as a "filter" through which the artworks would take shape in the design and layout of the exhibition. Delegating responsibility to an artist to make decisions about the installation meant that dynamics within the design of the exhibition occurred that may not have been possible had the curator taken sole responsibility. The same is true of *Utopia Station*, for which Rirkrit Tiravanija realized the exhibition design and Liam Gillick designed the seating. There are numerous other examples of artists—such as Julie Ault, Martin Beck, Judith Barry, and Josef Dabernig—who work as exhibition designers with curators.

16 Manifesta, Europe's "Nomadic Biennial," appoints a new group of curators, who have not necessarily worked together previously for each iteration. See https://manifesta.org/ (accessed March 20, 2023). For further information on documenta 11, for which Enwezor worked together with Carlos Basualdo, Ute Meta Bauer, Susanne Ghez, Sarat Maharaj,

Mark Nash, and Octavio Zaya, see https://www.documenta-archiv.de/en/documenta/118/11 and https://www.documenta-platform6.de/ (accessed March 20, 2022). For the 50th Biennale di Venezia, Francesco Bonami invited a range of other curators to curate a section of the Arsenale, which according to one of the curators involved "pushed plurality as far as possible."

17 Quite a few of these are discussed in essays in the following critical anthologies: Paul O'Neill, Simon Sheikh, Lucy Steeds, Mick Wilson, eds., *Curating after the Global: Roadmaps for the Present* (Cambridge, MA: MIT Press/CCS Bard,/Luma Foundation, 2019); and Paul O'Neill, Lucy Steeds, and Mick Wilson, eds., *How Institutions Think: Between Contemporary Art and Curatorial Discourse* (Cambridge, MA: MIT Press, 2017).

18 See, for instance, Irit Rogoff, "Smuggling—A Curatorial Model," in *Under Construction: Perspectives on Institutional Practice*, ed. Vanessa Joan Müller and Nicolaus Schafhausen (Cologne: Walther König, 2006), 132–33; Maria Lind, "The Curatorial," *Artforum,* October 2009, 103–05; Beatrice von Bismarck, "Curatorial Criticality: On the Role of Freelance Curators in the Field of Contemporary Art," in *Curating Critique*, ed. Marianne Eigenheer (Frankfurt: Revolver, 2007), 62–69; Emily Pethick, "The Dog that Barked at the Elephant in the Room," *The Exhibitionist*, no. 4, 2010; Paul O'Neill, "The Curatorial Constellation and the Paracuratorial Paradox," *The Exhibitionist*, no. 6, 2012; "Curating/Curatorial: A Conversation between Irit Rogoff and Beatrice von Bismarck," in *Cultures of the Curatorial*, ed. Beatrice von Bismarck, Jörn Schafaff, and Thomas Weski

(Berlin: Sternberg Press, 2012); Jean-Paul Martinon, ed., *The Curatorial: A Philosophy of Curating* (London: Bloomsbury, 2013).

19 See Charles Esche, "Curating and Collaborating: A Scottish Account," in *Stopping the Process?*, ed. Mika Hannula (Helsinki: nifca, 1998), 249.

20 One of Obrist's most often cited quotations in relation to the "educational turn." See, for example, Hal Foster, "Chat Rooms," in *Participation*, ed. Claire Bishop. (London/Cambridge, MA:

Whitechapel Gallery/ MIT Press, 2007), 194.

21 The increase of visibility of collective work is reflected in many recent publications, including the section on "Collectives," in *Mix & Stir: New Outlooks on Contemporary Art from Global Persepctives*, ed. Helen Westgeest and Kitty Zijlmans (Amsterdam: Valiz, 2021), *Texte zur Kunst*, issue 124, 2022, dedicated to "Collectivity," as well as the March 2023 issue of *frieze* on "collectives and cooperatives."

This is a significantly expanded, reedited, and updated version of a much shorter text called "Group Practice," first published in Art Monthly *in March 2007 and further developed for* Manifesta Journal, *2009–10 as "Beyond Group Practice."*

*W*eave, *Th*read, *N*ame...

Scenes of Collaboration

María Berríos / Pip Day / Sofía Olascoaga

What kinds of practices of citation, reciprocity, and solidarity are present in collaborative modes of working? In this exchange, we consider those that foreground the potential of collective energy, creativity, and diversity but that don't necessarily brand themselves as collaborative. We situate these against the dominant culture of individual authorship, which tends to bypass the acknowledgment, crediting, and naming of contributors.

This text is an exercise of collaborative thinking, which brings together examples drawn from personal experience and revisited anecdotes, informed by exhibitions, institutional contexts, and expanded artistic practice, both historical and current. The following is a rough compilation of questions and ideas around collectivity and collaboration woven together through several conversations over the past months although we have been in conversation, both direct through our work and by way of citation, for many years.

(I) To Hologram

Scene: Four people gather in a shopfront art space in Berlin. It's 2022, the Pirate Care Syllabus and Network have been widely accessed since early Covid days, and the Hologram has been active for a few years already.[1] The space is comfortable, we settle in. A fifth person welcomes the group, she will be guiding the day's experiment in gathering. We don't know each other, so the fifth invites us to introduce ourselves, but through movement, dance, a pose, gesture, or position, or through sound. She starts. We follow. We can see that we're all a little sick and that we all need a little help. For today, though, we decide together which one of us will be the "hologram" at the center of the "Hologram." Roles are then distributed: we decide who will be responsible as support for the "hologram's social well-being; her physical and material well-being; and her mental well-being." None of us are professional therapists, doctors, or social workers, lawyers, or bankers. We are all here to accompany and listen, rather than be a specialist.[2] The hologram is encouraged to find the tools to articulate her needs. On this day, she has a specific need and looks for a specific type of intervention. Ideas are bounced around. Together, the triangle forms an integrated approach. All areas of the hologram's life are implicated. And so, a group of strangers spends a few hours together, attempting to break the silence around struggling to maintain mental health and other kinds of everyday integral physical and social health.

And the hologram herself is not indebted to us, to her triangle. She's not obliged to give back. In fact, the Hologram as a structure erases the need for direct, immediate, or even future reciprocity: the transactional relationship is broken/unhinged. We are all unaccustomed to asking for help, and certainly not without feeling the obligation to reciprocate, but let's say that each hologram's triangle of people has their own triangle to lean on. The hologram, then, doesn't need to hesitate to ask, even when she is unable to reciprocate. And it's through this wide network of community resources—resources that are not provided in any other space by the State—that the expanded collaboration is achievable. This is interesting as a model for collaboration, or what can be understood as collaboration, and as an alternative extended network for the work of disentangling ourselves from the capitalist infrastructures that have made us ill in the first place.

A collaborative network that begins by creating a structure of reciprocity, or a network system where the need for reciprocity is vital when thinking through past and present collaborative practices, too often ends up in exhaustion and burn-out. Such a structure challenges us to consider how "collaborative" curatorial practices tend to frame themselves and the values they bring forth. For so many years, placing the participants' vital energy as a kind of sacrificial offering was a fundamental part and sustenance of the "collective," but frequently that sacrifice was unequally distributed, individualized, and often falling to women. This was the unspoken case with separatist women's groups in antipsychiatry in the 1970s, where the co-ed "group work" kept taking a toll on the women, whose issues would often be left less attended to. The mixed groups were able to somehow move beyond the psychiatric ideology wherein only the specialized disciplinary approach is able to deal with the complexity of a person's psyche—which was a huge move in terms of power dynamics—but they were not able to deal with the more structural burden of the care work that was unequally distributed in terms of gender and could only be addressed by fleeing.

(II) Mobile Academies or Curatorial as Editorial

Scene: She was a brilliant essayist and thinker, a self-taught educator. She managed to work sometimes in academic circles, but mostly she and her friends and colleagues would gather for smoky reading groups in her home, where they would discuss issues important to them. This was a kind of school for them, the only kind that could exist amid the censorship, and particularly the self-censorship, of the

dictatorship. The discussions were heated and the material
that came in would always, invariably, be photocopies, in
French or English, sometimes so faded that one would have
to use a sharp pencil to redraw the missing letters to make
out the words. Faded slides of relevant art also made their
way to the encounters, and often the artists participating
in the porous group would, sometimes fearfully, share their
works-in-progress with the group. Making exhibitions was
a rare privilege, it was the space for collective display,
exchange, and discussion of those things urgent to them.
Those collective readings and exchanges ultimately turned
into periodical publications that would come out when
possible, and would circulate hand to hand, becoming
a crucial reference point and mobile academy for the local
intellectual and artistic milieu. The reading groups and
references were collective, the energy too, but somehow
there was an unevenness that became more and more
heavily reliant on her. She had become a kind of matriarch,
and when she was tired enough, the dictatorship over,
and when their collective energy—half from those who
came in and out, and half hers—had waned along with their
independent agency to do things (as these things were,
by now, being done by the universities), she decided to call
it a day. Her leaving meant the entire collective endeavor
collapsed. It turned out, as is often the case in these
collective affairs, that there is indeed an individual motor,
keeping everything running, a kind of positive autocracy
of resistance.[3]

There is something relevant in collaboration, in collaborative practices,
which has to do with space, what is done where, what can be
done where. This is obvious in the need for and use of separatist
spaces, or in the case of cultural and artistic collaborative work done
in domestic spaces—which is always someone's space, someone's
kitchen—and how that changes the conversation or allows
a conversation to happen. Often that space is a space of labor for
someone, a space that, in order to operate as a space to share
things, wears that someone down. This has clear repercussions
when considering the spatial politics of exhibition-making.

(III) A Herd: The Makers

Scene: It is 1967 and a young writer wearing jeans and a white T-shirt is lying on a tiny corner of a large double bed; she is on her back holding an issue of *Playboy* magazine. Polluting the rest of the messy bedspread are magazines, paper bags, and other unidentifiable publications. She is in her room of the Hotel Nacional of Havana, where she has lived for several months while preparing an ambitious exhibition that will occupy the Pabellón Cuba in the Vedado neighborhood in the Cuban capital. She is on a mission to find images to be used in a large-scale anticolonial and anti-imperialist exhibition. She is part of a group of young Cuban revolutionaries that made a proposal to the central committee about the need to make a collective art show for the 1968 Cultural Congress of Havana—not just a sum of individualities, like in the 1967 Salon de Mayo and its celebrated large spiral "collective" mural where every artist painted a small square, but rather a collaborative artistic work. In this exhibition, there will be no single painter, no head architect, just cultural workers making a collectively conceived and executed exhibition. The "how" was something the group discussed at length. Why was it that in the visual arts there was this need for individual authorship and ownership? How did this need relate to the colonial and imperialist extraction of culture and images? They would reclaim what was theirs, in a reversal of centuries of looting of the cultural wealth of darker nations: they would loot the settlers' precious images and their "masters'" because the culture the empire claimed for itself, claimed as its property, belonged to everyone. Why was making an exhibition not considered a group effort, like in theater or cinema? The collective of young exhibition-makers were carpenters, electricians, script writers, model-makers, sound technicians, photographers, designers, editors. They modeled their exhibition as a film, as a kind of mechanical theater, where the "backstage" collective intelligence and work was acknowledged. "Working together we discussed *everything*, we became a herd."[4]

The Third World exhibition did have a collective working space: it was a small shop, in the building next to the Pavilion, a few steps away from the exhibition space where the group would meet to "cook" the exhibition together. They would sit around rather elaborate models they built to level the ground, so that they would all have the same kind of access to the work. In a way, they brought the kitchen to the foreground: the infrapolitical space of the invisibilized makers became a shared space, where everyone's knowledge had a role and was valued. This space for thinking through the exhibition together was as important to them as the exhibition space itself. The exhibition credit was for the "herd": they were all named, they felt no need to distinguish "collaborative" roles—such as artist, educator, curator, theorist—from supposedly technical ones—such as carpenter, sound technician, guard, cleaner. They were all cultural workers making an exhibition together, using art, as they stated, "as a means for decolonization." For them, art was a method, not a discipline-based practice. The exhibition space was, in this sense, an experiment in radical hospitality; it too needed to acknowledge the diverse collective social body of the audience, where what was offered should have a transgenerational appeal, and should address the specialist, the intellectual, the worker, and the housewife.

(IV) Hospitality, Mothering, and The Administrator

It is quite beautiful to follow the trajectory of artist Andrea Francke's work, where one can move from the transformation of the exhibition space into the nursery that the very same institution had deemed redundant, to creating a long-term collaborative conversation that was able to transfigure the bureaucratic process of evaluation into a space of hospitality. As far as I recall, to remake relevant furniture for the nursery she learned carpentry— following some manuals belonging to Latin American self-education collectives in the 1970s. Somehow, there are very material traces of her following the threads of the increasingly immaterial infrastructure involved in exhibition-making. For her, infrastructure always seems to become a practice of mutual exposure and encounter, ultimately a place for posing questions together. She approaches artistic practice always in relation to the act of instituting, pointing at the ways in which infrastructure makes those processes happen. She makes herself at home in that odd bureaucratic, often immaterial interspace, and invites others in, making sure they feel welcome even if the space or situation is uncomfortable or strange. She has a way of making tangible the scaffolding, the moments and the subjects of the infrastructural. As she states:

> Administrators become infrastructure not only through how their work is constructed and described, but also by how institutions are organised and narrated around an individual leader or hero. Administrative systems are collective by nature. Collective systems without shared aims, authorship or intent are as much of a challenge to organisations as they are to discourse. In order to attribute intention and purpose to a group, we either create competitive structures that elevate protagonists, heroes and leaders, or we institutionalise the collective so that it behaves like a coherent individual—attributing it ownership of its actions and products.[5]

Much like "infrastructure," the substrate is foundational, but it can be thought of as less "fixed"—in the imagination—than infrastructure, which those in power who benefit from current ones would have us believe is immutable or unchangeable. There is a very simple and telling example of how these dynamics work: James Scott wrote a work on peasant uprisings, basically demonstrating how that center-stage perspective of the protagonist is a very partial and performative—exhibitionist, we could say—form of history-telling.[6] The actual workings for that heroic moment come from what he calls the infrapolitical, the backstage, those places where power is not listening. The example he gives is that moment of injustice that is experienced and not contested, because nothing would be achieved in that specific center-stage moment, but later, in the barracks, among friends, the way the scene could have been played out is rehearsed over and over—what could have been said and done, improved, heightened, transmuted. Those scripts, that rehearsal, that ongoing and long-term chatter is the infrapolitics, and that is what eventually changes the infrastructure—not the moment of exposition. It would be very useful to think about reciprocity within the proportions of these unseen and silenced processes. Reciprocity should be considered and thought about in the context of infra-structures and substrates, and in the practice of protocols, a place where we can each begin to make relations.

(V) Underground

Scene A: A workforce of passionate humans resides for months, and then years, in the basement of a family house. They pedal every day, and night, to keep up the production of electricity going through fixed cycling devices, needed to power the lights at the top of the house. On the top floor, a small family enjoys the comforts of their pedal-powered television, domestic appliances, and always available electric light, thanks to the dozens of men, women, and children who believe that their workforce is a necessary defense during a long-extended war. The family that lives on the top floor had initially offered the basement as shelter, for the protection of people who had fled their homes because of the—originally real—war. After realizing the potential uses of human force under their floor, the family decided to stage a fake continuation of the war (through sound and light effects, and other tricks), and keep up the pantomime to allow their benefit of energy to continue, at the expense of—and through the ignorance and deceit of—the undergrounders, whose collective power used to light the enjoyment of a few.

Scene B: The billboard of a museum announces exhibitions on view: sober designs of images, and precise amounts of text, showing title and dates, and usually, credit to artist(s) and curator. The regimes of visibility in cultural production and in art institutions, tend to be faithful to traditions of citation, derived from Western notions of authorship.

Simultaneously, large groups of staff, professionally specialized, keep up with the administrative, logistic, operative, production, conservation, communication, design, education, maintenance, edition, publishing, promotion, legal, archiving, documenting, reviewing, guarding, securing, and volunteering, around the programming of the gallery exhibitions. Sometimes, or rather often, working premises are also *underground*, where staff is located and focused on keeping up the pristine and well-lit white cube galleries that hold the artistic statements of specific forms of authorial work above.

We witness the tendency to flatten the complexities of power, citation, and acknowledgment under reductive notions of *collaboration*, that blur, invisibilize, and hierarchize diverse subjectivities and forms of labor. In the face of the precarity of cultural labor, normalized notions of value production continue to render invisible forms of essential labor that interconnect and support the very real context of cultural production. This happens in the knowledge that this precarity, however, is relative to other forms of extremely exploitative labor outside the cultural sector.

(VI) Work, Work, Work, Work

Scene: Maintenance and cleaning Drink coffee (or beer) with artists Attend openings and inaugurations Go to parties Organize parties and fundraising activities Find services, money, and donated materials Prepare budgets and timetables Complete accountability reports Design strategic plans Answer the phone Open and close the door Turn the exhibition lights on and off Turn the exhibition's audiovisual equipment on and off Buy books for the library and keep them organized Write a lot of emails Produce videoconferences Prepare reports for the Administrative Board Meet with the Administrative Board Attend foundations' events and meetings Develop and sustain relations with foundations' personnel and donors Organize birthday lunches for collaborators Recharge the

rechargeable batteries Coordinate the exhibitions' install
and deinstall Offer guided tours Talk about the organization
Change the defect lightbulbs Fix the microwave Set up
the space for events: place the chairs, take out the tables
Open and close the windows Water the plants Buy food
for the workshops' coffee breaks Brew tons of coffee Cook
Buy materials for the workshops Recruit participants for
the workshops Confirm their attendance Scan documents
Prepare FedEx and DHL shipments Go to the post office
Take inventories of equipment and furnishings Keep the
storage room organized and keep track of loaned equipment
Coordinate guests' pickups from the airport Turn the
alarm on and off Be the emergency contact for the alarm
monitoring company Make copies of and monitor the
keys to the space Curate exhibitions Write art books Buy
materials for artists to create their pieces Read applications
for open calls Produce and share social media content
Make stories during the events Document Talk about the
work that is being done Produce publications Distribute
publications Produce podcasts Loan the space to others
Sweep, dust, clean the tables Look after international
guests Hang out with guests and take them out on trips
and strolls Offer critique, references, and resources Advise,
connect, be aware of who is doing what Visit studios
and exhibitions, take others with you Internal meetings
Meetings with collaborators Meetings with people who walk
in the door Buy paper Buy ink Take care of the seller of
printers Call and follow up with the plumber Fumigate with
regularity and talk with the exterminator Monitor cracks and
leaks Shoo the cats Talk with the neighbors Save parking
spaces Graphic design Editing Printing Programming
Call the printing press Go to the printing press Talk with
technical support Proofreading Residencies Write Read
Mediate Negotiate Forgive Soft diplomacy Write press
releases and send them Make every effort for the press to
cover something Update the website Deal with hackers
Meetings in Zoom Prepare and offer classes, workshops,
talks Make grants and other forms of economic support
happen for the organization and its collaborators Make

grants and other forms of economic support happen for us
as artists Disseminate information on grants and resources
Translate Offer orientation to international curators Make
foreign foundations familiar with "the cultural ecosystem"
Do the dishes Clean the toilet Replenish the toilet paper
Pay the rent Pay the electricity, water, and internet bills Pay
collaborators Negotiate our pay Pay ourselves Participate
in WhatsApp chats.[7]

How can diverse modes of collaboration redefine and challenge
the very contours of individualized practice, while also untangling
notions of professionalization? How does the desire to merge
into shared processes challenge the imposed professional roles as
defined in academic, institutional, and cultural terms, rather than
through process itself? In the work of exhibition-making, as publics
bring another dimension to reciprocity in collaboration, contours
can be even further expanded. We look to cases where publics have
become integral to the process, as part of the expanded collective,
actively welcomed into collectivity, and where blurring the dividing
line of active/maker and passive/receiver is prioritized.

(VII) An Exhibition That Flowed with the Street

Scene: The exhibition the group of young Cuban
revolutionaries worked on was conceived for the 1968
Cultural Congress of Havana, a meeting of Third
World intellectuals and their allies, a cultural Bandung,
a tricontinental examination of revolutionary culture.
For the young exhibition-makers this meant that it had
to be an exhibition not only for the over 1,000
intellectuals, writers, poets, filmmakers, but also for
the housewife, the worker, the student… for all cultural
workers, as everyone who contributed to the revolution
also contributed to its culture: being made *by* a collective
would also mean made *for* the collective, a popular
space for intergenerational and international exchange.
There was a flashing three-dimensional neon sign
that read "Del Tercer Mundo" that could be seen all

along the block in the front garden of the Pabellón
Cuba, where loudspeakers called out into the famous
walking strip of La Rambla: "Welcome to the Third World
exhibition." The exhibition opened in the early evening
so that the light effects could be appreciated: a spectacle
that could embrace the workers on their way home,
catch the attention of the groups of school kids on their
late afternoon strolls, a place for the *pioneritos* being
taken home from school by their mothers. There were
even two lions and a llama borrowed from the zoo.
Once in the Pabellón Cuba, a half building-half garden,
a soundtrack pulled the audience through the different
narrative zones of the exhibit. In the first weeks, the
exhibition had over 100,000 visitors. The official count,
two months later, claimed 250,000 visitors in total.[8]

"Collaboration" as a term has been used to flatten diversity, friction,
and the power dynamics behind collective and institutional cultural
production, projecting only particular hierarchies of crediting, while
invisibilizing and normalizing the erasure of structural, geopolitical,
and economic realities as well as the inequalities of international
cultural production as a complex and widely collectivized force.
We ask: how could a practice of responsive listening, articulated
through a commitment to reciprocity, shift the inertias and normalized
ways of valuing (or diminishing) cultural and artistic work? And,
in turn: How could this impact our capacity as cultural workers to
acknowledge, credit, and relate to the diverse modes of creating
value and meaning in our context?

(VIII) Exhibition-Making as a School for Urban Rebellion

Scene: In 1969, it was declared that the Inter-American
Bank would grace the city of Valparaíso with a vast amount
of money to connect their port to the port of Mendoza-
Argentina through an ambitious "modernizing" highway
project that would rip through the port's coastline: the
Via Elevada. Since the 1950s, teachers and students at
the local architecture school had been realizing poetic

actions and concrete art exhibitions, as well as poetic journeys across Latin America. For them, all of this was a way to develop collective methodologies on how to inhabit and transform their territories, and their city, which was considered their learning laboratory. For them it was about creating a kind of urban "intimacy." When the *Via Elevada* project was announced, the entire school mobilized and their poetic promenades became a huge silent protest "against the Urbanicide of the Via Elevada." The entire school paralyzed all other activities and turned their energies into collectively developing an alternative project that they called *Avenida del Mar*, which would respect the tempo of a city whose rhythm is that of the coast. Students and teachers worked together for a year with local neighborhood organizations and guilds, they called in other professionals to help develop a collective counter-project. The local government authorities did finally give the school an initial deadline but ended up not responding, effectively ignoring them. The response of the Architecture school was to make a large "exhibition" that opened on the day of the initial deadline for their counterproposal. They hung large wooden panels along the streets explaining the process and the project, inviting people to the exhibition location where a huge Merzbau-like maquette of the city of Valparaíso crawled up the walls and peeked out of windows. They invited the entire city, the mayor, and even the President, who did not show up. Students, teachers, fishermen, neighbors, and sociologists gave talks and discussed the proposed project on display.

Everybody's talking about reciprocity. We're interested in seeing where practices of reciprocity are taking place and cases where it operates as the locus and mechanism for putting into practice the much-needed structural change that everyone is also talking about. Curatorial practice itself is, at the best of times, founded on reciprocal methodologies and practices, while it is used to maintain asymmetries of power at the worst of times. We are specifically interested in how we can establish protocols for and guides toward working reciprocally—that is, as form, ethically, and incorporating fluidity—to work on an undoing or rebalancing of those asymmetries that have been inherited and upheld by those in positions of power and privilege.

(IX) Collaboration as Re-distribution

As the pandemic hit, and people began to lose their jobs, the Indigenous Curatorial Collective / Collectif des commissaires autochtones (ICCA) reacted quickly with an Emergency Response Fund: "send us a two-minute video, and we'll give you a hundred bucks." Through the ICCA funding efforts, $100 turned into $1,000, and the collective would go on to re-distribute $435,000 (Canadian) to Indigenous practitioners as part of their Curating Care (later Community Cares) program across Canada.[9]

Part of a wider approach to supporting Indigenous artists and curators, the ICCA's then team—Camille Georgeson-Usher (Executive Director) and Camille Larivée (Director of Programs)—sought to address the issues of needy infrastructure in arts institutions across Canada at the substrate level. On the one hand, ICCA lent extensive support to Indigenous-led organizations and the curators and artists they work with. With respect to non-Indigenous organizations, ICCA's task was a complex and involved one. As the Canada Council for the Arts began to ask institutions to report on the ethnicity of their staff, board, artists, curators, and other collaborators they worked with—which roughly coincided with the recommendations of the Truth and Reconciliation Commission report (2015) and the Canadian government's launch of a campaign of "reconciliation" between "Canada" and Indigenous peoples—museums and other organizations across the country began to put out calls specifically for Indigenous hires, without, however, preparing the institutions or their mostly white staffs for the specific cultural needs and practices that would emerge.

In response, the ICCA established a membership program that functioned as both a site for education on an institutional level, and as a safeguard for Indigenous practitioners looking to work in these institutions. Museums were encouraged by the ICCA to look at their policies and practices, and to articulate their approach to—and reasons for—their particular hire. Coupled with mentorship initiatives like that of the Montreal Arts Council's Indigenous programs—where funding was established to remunerate acting Indigenous mentors to newly hired Indigenous curators at institutions in Montreal—the ICCA's approach went a long way in securing healthier working conditions. The ICCA does not articulate its approach in the language of the government's framework of "reconciliation" but rather as resurgence and self-determination: "The ICCA activates Indigenous creative sovereignty, ensuring future ancestors have agency over their own cultures as an Inherent Right."[10]

In the effort to gather relevant scenes of collaboration, in the attempt to move toward acknowledged practices of sovereignty, reciprocity, and solidarity, we follow many women we admire whose academic, political, literary, and practice-based work foregrounds women who have historically been unacknowledged, un-cited, under-celebrated, or indeed, actively written out of archives. (I remember the privilege of sitting in a workshop between two women poets, one whispering in each ear, in different languages—neither my native tongue—pencil and paper in hand, trying to collect some of the gifted words). But of course they refuse to stay put. They pass through us, beside us, that pluriversity of women who are foundational to the substrates and infrastructures we need, their movements past and present, their discussions over kitchen tables, the archives under their beds and in boxes stored in closet shelves, the stories they share and propagate. We can only try and keep up. By continuously reshaping questions they are protocol-building… responding.

(X) Responding[11]

V

a voice stutters in the background of our waking mind

[generic possessive pronoun] stutter is our stutter

or it is the way we define our difference?

                                        stutter is nation

beneath an image of human figures the words

[you have nothing to lose but your chains

                              at times two voices talk to one another

                              [generic human] faces [tired]

we know we are all constructed

when it comes down to it we don't believe it

the social always holds us back

while the ways that we encounter relation are various

we remain

searching [searching

we question, respond

[deny we [move forward

1   Cassie Thornton and Lita Wallis describe the Hologram as "an open-source, peer-to-peer, viral social technology for dehabituating humans from capitalism." A Hologram consists of a group of four people: a triangle of support around the central person, or "hologram." See https://syllabus. pirate.care/topic/hologramsocialcare/ (accessed March 16, 2023).

2   The Hologram's peer-to-peer model is not concerned with advice or "treatment," but the triangle does support decision-making at times. Over the long term, for example, it may attempt to relieve the burden around parsing medical opinions or the economic effects of living with a medical or other condition that would otherwise typically fall on one person. The Hologram creates a different way of relating or weaving together aspects around health that are not purely treatment oriented.

3   This was the case for well-known critical journals produced outside the academic realm in Chile and Argentina, which began during or in the post-dictatorial context around women like Nelly Richard or Beatriz Sarlo. In a similar way, it could describe the journey of the Cuban magazine *Criterios*, with the sole difference that it was dedicated entirely to translations, made by a wonderful polyglot cultural critic who passed away in 2017, Desiderio Navarro.

4   For further information on the 1968 Cultural Congress of Havana and the Third World Exhibition, see María Berríos and Jakob Jakobsen, "Archives, Struggles, and Exhibitions," in *Curating after the Global: Roadmaps for the Present*, ed. Paul O'Neill, Simon Sheikh, Lucy Steeds,

and Mick Wilson (Cambridge MA: MIT Press, 2019), 229–51.

5   Andrea Francke and Ross Jardine, "Bureaucracy's Labor: The Administrator as Subject," *PARSE Journal*, issue 5, spring 2017, available at https://parsejournal.com/ article/bureaucracys-labour-the-administrator-as-subject/ (accessed March 15, 2023).

6   James Scott, *The Moral Economy of the Peasant: Rebellion and Subsistence in Southeast Asia* (New Haven: Yale University Press, 1981).

7   Derived from the "Work" section in *Introduction to the Employee Handbook,* an anti-handbook for cultural workers. In it we aim to share strategies of resistance, camouflaging techniques, and methods to counterbalance precarious working conditions and neoliberal strategies that instrumentalize art and culture in contexts with fragile institutions. It is a joint effort between TEOR/ éTica, Beta-Local (PR) and Taller de Ediciones Económicas (MEX) with the purpose of thinking together about the employment rights we demand, and what type of workers we aspire to be. "Introducción al Manual del Empleade," *Teorética*, Beta Local, Taller de Ediciones Económicas, 2022. Available at https://teoretica. org/producto/introduccion-al-manual-del-empleade/ (accessed March 16, 2023).

8   See Berríos and Jakobsen, "Archives, Struggles, and Exhibitions."

9   See https://icca.art/community-cares-part-2-2023/ (accessed March 15, 2023).

10   See https://icca.art/ (accessed March 15, 2023).

11   Juliana Spahr, "Responding" from *Response* (excerpt). Copyright © 1996 Juliana Spahr.

Detecting / Distilling Care in Curating / the Curatorial

Bonaventure Soh Bejeng Ndikung

In thinking about the delusion of care there is a need to think self-critically about my own field—curating and curatorial practice. Curators are fond of linking their practices to the etymology of the verb *curate*, derived from the Latin *curare*, "to take care of," and the word *curator*, a person responsible for care, derived from the past participle *curatus*. It is understandable that curators—as well as directors of museums, galleries, or art exhibitions—relate their practices to ideas of "looking after," which is certainly in some way about care. But here too, I would like us to take some time to think about what this "taking care" in curating might actually mean in practice.

My primary concern stems from what I call the "curatorial complex." The "curatorial complex" is the tendency whereby almost everything is carefully trimmed to fit the orbit of the metaphor. Especially in contemporary independent curating, not only is many a subject dealt with metaphorically, the notion of care is also positioned as something that is fundamental to curating, and curatorial practice tends to be reduced to that realm of the metaphor. This is not to problematize using figures of speech to describe things or actions. Quite to the contrary: metaphors enrich artistic works textually and aesthetically, and in using metaphors we can simplify and make accessible and comprehensible some very complicated notions. Take for example "time is money," or "the world's a stage": while "money" and "stage" aid us significantly in understanding the complexity of time and the world, respectively, it would be problematic to reduce time only to money and the world only to being a stage. My first concern with the "curatorial complex" though is that many descriptions of what curating entails simplify care to a seemingly self-explanatory metaphor. In an era in which curating has come to mean everything and nothing, and is often reduced to the sheer act of selecting and a matter of choice and display, Jean-Paul Martinon and Irit Rogoff 's proposed definition of *the curatorial* serves as a welcome expansion of the field and what it is capable of:

> If "curating" is a gamut of professional practices that had to do with setting up exhibitions and other modes of display, then "the curatorial" operates at a very different level: it explores all that takes place on the stage set-up, both intentionally and unintentionally, by the curator and views it as an event of knowledge. So to drive home a distinction between "curating" and "the curatorial" means to emphasize a shift from the staging of the event to the actual event itself: its enactment, dramatisation and performance.[1]

This is of particular interest because by employing the notion of the curatorial, one *expands* the "space" of care from selection and display to also encompass *enactment, dramatization, and performance.* By this, I understand that all "events" that were considered extracurricular to curating—such as discursive programs, symposia, public programs, performances, reading spaces, and more—are actually crucial components of the exhibition itself wherein the artworks and topics at stake are surrounded by manifold trajectories of exploration. In considering all that is staged and treating this as an "event of knowledge" through varying channels and mediums, provisions are made for the artist, the art, and the exhibitionary frameworks in terms of presentation, maintenance, cultivation, protection, dissemination, mediation, and other epistemic, moral, and legal considerations that one could call "care."

Though the curatorial offers a widened space of care for the practice, in thinking about curating/the curatorial, I had to think about the debates on *Créolité* versus Creolization. Not in content or meaning, but in the framework of the processual, and in the relation of the static versus dynamic embedded in the concepts of *Créolité* versus Creolization, respectively. When Manthia Diawara asked Édouard Glissant about *Créolité* aboard the Queen Mary II in 2009, Glissant responded that:

> When you say "Créolité" you fix its definition of being once and for all in time and place. Now I think that being is in a state of perpetual change. And what I call creolisation is the very sign of that change. In creolisation, you can change, you can be with the Other, you can change with the Other while being yourself, you are not one, you are multiple, and you are yourself. You are not lost because you are multiple. You are not broken apart because you are multiple. Créolité is unaware of this. It becomes another unity like Frenchness, Latinity, etc., etc. That is why for a long time now I have developed the idea of creolisation, which is a permanent process that supersedes historical avatars.[2]

I am interested in thinking about curating in a state of perpetual change, in a process, curating as a multiple concept that develops and adjusts itself in time and space. With the notion of the curatorial I see an adjustment in function, but one that comes across still as static in space and time. With what I would like to call *curatorialization* I propose the possibility of a curatorial practice that is malleable in form, space, and time, that in its multiplicity of existences expands the scope of curatorial practice itself. In this case, instead of understanding the music selection process of the DJ in a club as an act of curating, one could imagine a curator implementing the working method of the DJ within a process of making an exhibition, which is to say, thinking of the audience of the exhibition like a DJ would think of the dancers on the dance floor. This necessitates

a deep understanding of the space, deep listening to the bodies
that occupy the space, and a deep mastery of responding to the way
moods change with time across an evening of a DJ set. There
is a constant adaptation taking place. As soon as the DJ notices that
the floor has come to a standstill, they need to react, they need to
catch the attention of the dancers and need to keep them on the move.

In using this analogy to exemplify what I mean by
curatorialization, I am in no way trying to equate the curator to
a DJ, but I am trying to imagine ways of expanding the field of care of
the curator's practice—a care for the artist and art, but also a deep
sense of care for the audience at the disposition of the curator.
What I am proposing is that besides moving from the act of just
display/staging (curating) to enacting, dramatizing, and performing
events of knowledge (the curatorial), curatorialization would also
have to mean employing other strategies that open up cracks and
caveats of care that we may not have explored until now, and that
constantly adapt themselves to the needs of the artists, the art,
and audiences, as well as times and spaces—and most especially
over extended periods of time before and beyond the exhibition
itself. Exhibitions are often always conceived as static entities, but
it is this thinking of an exhibition and finding ways of vivifying an
exhibition, its processes before, during, and after the act—display,
staging performances, and symposia—that I would like to think
of as curatorialization.

For those of us who carry the burdens of historical
disenfranchisement, I would like to push that notion of curatorialization
to also relate to the notion of *marronage*. In the binary of "fight or
flight," it is often fight that is considered the active form of resistance.
But in the history of slavery in the Caribbean and Latin American
slave enterprises—in Barbados, Brazil, Jamaica, or Suriname, but
also in the Indian ocean, for example in La Reunion—*marronage*
served as a possibility for slaves to escape from plantations and
create maroon communities on the peripheries of these enterprises:
be it the "*petit marronage*," in which people escaped for a short period
of time to then return, or "*grand marronage*," in which they escaped
permanently. At the heart of it all were strategies of resistance, which
sometimes led to rebellions across some colonies. In their hideouts,
the marooned could challenge the plantation system by the sheer
fact of being absent, depriving the plantation of its workforce, by

attacking the plantations, or negotiating their freedom and autonomy, but also encouraging or inciting others to follow suit. What is also fascinating about the act and space of *marronage* is the ability to retreat—both as a concept of pulling back and as a notion of caring for oneself and one's kin. In my proposal of curatorialization as *marronage*, I would like to imagine a space like SAVVY Contemporary in Berlin, Khiasma in Paris, RAW Material Company in Dakar, just to name a few, as spaces of retreating. Not as metaphor, but as a way of organizing, congregating peoples, knowledges, and things we care about and intend to care for.

Another example of an effort of extending that space of the curatorial and thereby offering care beyond the metaphor can be observed in Jonas Tinius and Sharon Macdonald's essay "The Recursivity of the Curatorial." Irrespective of the historical short-comings of anthropology as a discipline, and problems inherent to its practices, it is worth taking a glance at Tinius and Macdonald's proposal and the relation between anthropology and curatorial practice in the following excerpts:

> Recursivity differs from reflexivity. Reflexivity refers to reflection on one's own position, and in our research contexts could indicate anthropologists coming to new understandings of themselves through reflecting on others, or other people thinking about anthropologists and thus coming to understanding themselves. Recursivity, however, is about a "recursive sequence of revelation" in which the relation between two perspectives "is constantly redefining the partners in the exchange, the objects of exchange, and the very concept of exchange" (Sansi 2018: 123). As such, recursivity is performative and implies action. It refers to an ongoing mutually-affecting relationality between things, people, thoughts, and forms of knowledge. This is not just a combination of reflexive processes but the generation of something new. [...] Yet, there are specific ways in which this recursive generation of knowledge plays out in different fields. In the case of the relation between anthropology and curating, and to return to the mirror-image metaphor of the ricochet effects of recursivity, we are dealing with a socio-epistemic exchange.[3]

There are two things I would like to take with me from this proposal of the recursive, as holding potential to enable spaces of care, which are: a) this relation of perspectives—between things, people, thoughts, and forms of knowledge, between disciplines like curating and anthropology—that end up being more than the sums of the parts that make up the relation; and b) the socio-epistemic exchange that can be generated from such relations and spaces—where the elements of the relation also emerge, evolve and become as a result of the exchange.

That said, one must be careful with the trend of "curator as ethnographer" that we often stumble across. Due to obvious limits in time and funding, curators tend to delve rather superficially into certain subjects. In the past decades, in which we observed Western curators wanting to do exhibitions on artists from the non-West—especially after the revolts in North Africa—one has observed that a curator from New York, for example, would fly to Cairo for three days, come back, and do an exhibition about Egyptian art. My colleagues and I, too often, get emails from curator colleagues with the question "I am working on XYZ, please send me a list of African artists working on these issues." It is not a problem to seek advice from colleagues per se, but when this becomes a methodology, it is problematic. There is something about such examples of curatorial "research" that feel as if shopping for artists in a supermarket. Such approaches are concerning, because there is no attempt to enter into a profound conversation and relationship with these artists, and care falls by the wayside. This practice of "remote curating," wherein a curator sits at their desk in place A and works with artists in place B without ever doing a studio visit, even just online, is part of this trend of the "curator as ethnographer." Too often the result is the production of epistemic violence through the practice of exhibition-making, as the complex sociopolitical or aesthetic phenomena with which many artists are concerned can neither be discerned within three days of visiting forty artists in Pakistan or Cairo, nor through an online studio visit. Too often this leads to yawning generalizations and unreliable assertions. The critique of bias often ascribed to ethnographers— as their practices tend to be dependent on particular informants, observations, and limits in comprehension—can also be applied to the "curator as ethnographer."

I would like to end with a note on caring and curing. In the whole fascination with the etymological link of curating to care, often the notion of *curare* as relating to "healing" is forgotten. Of course, it is quite a big claim to assert that art can offer a form of healing. But how else can we imagine curating as a process that may eventually lead to some kind of social or spiritual healing—not just of symptoms that surface, but a more holistic notion of healing that relates to the roots of our societal concerns and troubles?

1   Jean-Paul Martinon and Irit Rogoff, "Preface," in *The Curatorial: A Philosophy of Curating,* ed. Jean-Paul Martinon (London: Bloomsbury, 2013), ix.

2   Manthia Diawara and Édouard Glissant, "Conversation with Édouard Glissant Aboard the Queen Mary II" (August 2009).

3   Jonas Tinius and Sharon Macdonald, "The recursivity of the curatorial," in *The Anthropologist as Curator,* ed. Roger Sansi (London: Bloomsbury Academic, 2020), 42–43.

This essay has been significantly updated and edited from its original in Bonaventure Soh Bejeng Ndikung, The Delusion of Care *(Berlin: Archive Books, 2021), 45–55.*

Controlled Conversations

Agnieszka Pindera

The main protagonist of the comedic film trilogy of the Polish transformation period—Ryszard Ochódzki, President of the Rainbow sports club—falls victim to the dreadful absurdity typical for socialist countries. The unstable political climate that arrived with the end of socialism is depicted in the background of the series' many twists and turns. Throughout the first film, Ochódzki tries to access his foreign bank account before his soon-to-be-ex-wife does. Its sequel, titled *Controlled Conversations* (*Rozmowy kontrolowane* in Polish), is organized around events unfolding during government-imposed martial law. The title refers to a scene in which a call from a telephone booth is interrupted by a militia officer repeating a phrase typical of censorship: "controlled conversation." As the call progresses, the caller takes over the official's task and "self-censors" while the law-enforcement representative eats his sandwich.

This scene could be argued to represent the past and what we experience today in times of exhaustion—of both resources and outdated political systems. Currently the art world across Europe—like the caller in the scene—acts in place of defunct policies by taking over the role of state officials, all the while busying itself with fulfilling self-serving goals. Such turns, which are mainly exercised by collective curatorial initiatives, can be perceived as a voluntary desertion from the field of culture. As explained by Paweł Wodziński, representative of the Biennale Warszawa, getting closer to spheres of economy, politics, and social issues (i.e., providing support to unhoused people) allows one to distance oneself from the culture wars that by definition generate conflict and make collaboration impossible. At the same time, the rise of right-wing populism, nationalism, as well as other extreme positions—again similar to the Cold War era—makes audiences mistrust public cultural institutions and forces them to look for alternatives. In other words, demand calls for supply.

Biennale: Your Call Has Been Forwarded to an Automatic Voice Message System

The first initiative to flourish outside public art infrastructures in this part of Europe was the OFF-Biennale in Budapest, an international art event established in 2014 that has, since then, boycotted official Hungarian cultural policies.[1] All its founders worked in major museums, galleries, and universities in Budapest before these institutions were taken over by Viktor Orbán's regime. When a group of curators and scholars decided to lay the foundations for collaboration, it took a form of "prefigurative politics"—in which they collectively enacted the performance of an institution they'd wished was the norm.

The Biennale Warszawa grew out of seemingly different yet similar circumstances. It was a short-lived municipal establishment created in 2017–18 that closed in mid-2022. Not a biennial office, but an institution headed by Paweł Wodziński, an actor, director, and scenographer, which combined visual art and social activism, and operated on two-year thematic cycles. In the beginning, the Biennale Warszawa collectively curated a series of events that dealt with possible alternatives in organizing and instituting in the face of (global) neoliberal rules dominating social life and the rise of right-wing populism represented by the PiS party in Poland.[2]

By adopting the name "biennale" for their initiatives, both groups revealed their critical stance on regionalism and nationalism that the notion of "biennale" historically conveys. In the beginning, the OFF-Biennale aimed to amplify and coordinate many independent projects that were happening locally, as well as organize fundraising.[3] Eastern European countries depend fully on the state—either on direct state funding or international resources distributed by the state. The Hungarian curatorial collective behind the OFF-Biennale opposed the state's official agenda and decided to "monetize" their available resources, namely, the international network developed from its members' years of working in institutions. To be able to work on projects and avoid self-censorship they sought support from institutions and programs that didn't need state approval.[4] In other words, the OFF-Biennale managed to use its international connections to support free speech within the local art scene.

In the case of the Biennale Warszawa, the division between the state's wrongdoing and free grassroots culture isn't so clear, as the state's current leadership was formed by the municipal level of the opposition party. The curators were aware that a sense of locality had been reproduced for specific political reasons, and had been easily abused to stimulate isolationist ideas arising from a political agenda. To overcome such a threat, the Biennale Warszawa promoted, as they called it, progressive politics that are collaborative by default and based on relations on a transnational and trans-local scale. The Biennale Warszawa's most ambitious project was its participation in the 2021 Kyiv Biennial, which stood out as a model because of its identification of and acting upon regional concerns. That Kyiv Biennial curatorial team was drawn from the five organizations that formed the East Europe Biennial Alliance (EEBA). Among its members were teams of Biennale Warszawa and OFF-Biennale Budapest, as well as the host institution Kyiv Biennial, joined by the resurrected Biennale Matter of Art Prague, and the youngest member in the group, Survival Kit Festival Riga. At first, they organized gatherings in Prague, Warsaw, Palermo, as well as Kyiv, allowing the time and space to develop common goals. The group decided to test their ideas in practice through the joint organization of the fourth edition of Kyiv Biennial, titled *Allied*, in 2021.

While speaking about the exhibitions they curate, Alliance members tend to call them "forums," to distinguish their projects from more traditional modes of display. In the *School of Kyiv* edition (2015), for instance, the Kyiv Biennial involved cultural institutions across the city, including art schools, museums, and libraries, all allowing free admission to "arenas of public reflection."[5] These were organized around eight topics: The School of Abducted Europe, offering ideas for another Europe; The School of the Displaced, which gathered refugees; The School of Image and Evidence, which tackled the problem of propaganda; The School of Landscape, which discussed the relation between nationhood and land; The School of the Lonesome, which served activists who took part in Maidan; and The School of Realism. During its first edition, the Biennale Warszawa organized four conventions engaging with the following: issues of transnationalism (Transunions); the climate change emergency (Convention of Women Farmers); alternative aims to Polish foreign policies (East-European–North African–Middle East forum); and offering space for representatives of Polish non-governmental organizations to discuss ways to stimulate progressive social change.

Three biennial editions preceded *Allied*, starting with *School of Kyiv*. This first edition was organized the year after the Revolution of Dignity,[6] which resulted in new Ukrainian memory politics that introduced more restrictive decommunization laws—erasing any existing ties with the Soviet Union, including cultural liaisons and avant-garde traditions. The Kyiv Biennial organizers—the Visual Culture Research Center—were invested in restoring the heritage of the modern period in Ukrainian history, which they deemed emancipatory. In the words of the Visual Culture Center Director Vasyl Cherepanyn during his opening speech, contemporary Ukrainians could learn from that historical period how to be contemporary in other ways than by accepting neoliberal measures.[7] Interestingly, he connected the very local issues, which urgently needed to be resolved internally, with internationalism. Like the Poles, Ukrainians tend to be strongly anti-isolationist, as both nations have historically suffered from tight information control, manipulation, and propaganda.

What was being repeated in statements about these collective curatorial initiatives in Budapest and Kyiv was a need for a solid foundation. Uprisings end usually as rapidly as they start, and while such events ignite the search for new formations, these also need to be completed. To sustain change started by a movement, an institutional form has to crystallize and consolidate itself. As Cherepanyn put it in 2017, "an international collective of social and politically engaged institutions—that is the most important art piece we need today, in order to conduct real transnational politics." Consequently, the EEAB was formed by representatives from Poland, Ukraine, Czech Republic, Latvia, and Hungary, all countries that were previously under control of the Soviet regime. Three decades after regaining their individual identity as sovereign nations, they formed a collective, appropriating a once forced and phony transnationalism to counter new types of oppression.

Solidarity Community Center: In the Interest of Quality Control, Calls May Be Recorded. If You Do Not Agree with Being Recorded, Please Hang Up

"Sunflower" Solidarity Community Center in Warsaw was brought to life as an intervention to help refugees from Ukraine after the Russian invasion in 2022. It took its name from Ukraine's national flower—which was also incorporated into peculiar civil acts of resistance and protests taking place in the occupied territories—and started among many art professionals engaging in civil activities.[8] During this time, cultural institutions urgently re-purposed their resources, with residency programs opening their doors to those seeking shelter. Museums—thinking more long term—started to give free Polish language lessons to stimulate integration of the newcomers. Diverse communities organized help at overcrowded train stations, and managed free shops for refugees.[9] Many of these initiatives ceased to exist after a few months, as they were organized by citizens without proper training in crisis management. "Sunflower" is one of the few that hasn't exhausted its human resources, and its institutional affiliation may be what ensures its durability. Formally it was an artistic action organized by the Museum of Modern Art in Warsaw, and the collective that curated it was nominated in the visual arts category for an annual Polish cultural award, the Polityka's Passport. Initiated by Polish and Ukrainian artists, activists, and cultural professionals, among them members of the Blyzkist

Collective (Ukrainian for closeness) and curators of Warsaw MoMA, the group relied on the competence of others within the established network of collectives and NGOs to organize aid efficiently.[10]

What spontaneously fulfilled immediate needs at the beginning—feeding those who came by train, and, with MoMA's proximity to Warsaw Central station, taking pictures for legal documents to register for temporary protection in Poland, as well as caring for children while parents visited civil services to submit paperwork—evolved into symbiotic relationships with the art institutions it relied on. As the collective claims, the transformation of the museum into a civil center had historical precedents. What they call "solidarity-based" museology was put in place at the Malmö Art Museum in 1945, when it transformed into a home for female prisoners liberated from concentration camps. The same solidarity manifested in American museums organizing food banks at their headquarters during the Covid-19 pandemic.

When it no longer had to provide assistance to displaced people, as this role was taken over by other bodies, "Sunflower" took over the reins of the museum's public programming, organizing events aimed at enhancing Polish-Ukrainian relations—by teaching both languages, and providing information on Ukrainian art and culture through concerts, lectures, and screenings. The second program branch was devoted to the current war, Russian imperialism, and specific issues of decolonization in Eastern Europe. The collective is also engaged in the *Soniakh Digest* magazine—an international platform that discusses global consequences of the Russian invasion—and is working with the Kyiv Biennial on its 2023 and 2025 editions.[11] The "Sunflower" collective also shows solidarity with other social groups: for instance, together with street workers they organize meetings every Tuesday for people recovering from the homelessness crisis or who are at risk of becoming unhoused.

We're Sorry, You Have Reached a Number That Has Been Disconnected or Is No Longer in Service

The recipient of the controlled call described at the beginning of this text was a theater worker speaking in code. Hearing that "the Swedish bun has been bitten into and a fresh roll has to be delivered," she knew what needed to be done. It meant that Ryszard Ochódzki's cover had been blown, and he had to leave the country pretending to be a Scandinavian citizen, which might only work with the help of theater makeup artists. But in 1980s Eastern Europe conversations and borders were not the only spheres of life that were strictly controlled. Everything that entered the public domain— including art and culture—was supervised, and if not directly censored, economic crises and shortages did the job. More or less at the same time *Controlled Conversations* takes place, students of the Film School in Łódź —the Action Workshop collective—were fed up with the isolation imposed upon them by the socialist state and tried to overcome it. They managed to convince the Solidarność [Solidarity] Workers Union to become involved in an exhibition aiming to reevaluate international art of the 1970s, as it had been presented by official museum exhibitions. *Construction in Process* gathered work of fifty-four artists in a large industrial space in Łódź that served as the show's venue. Instead of shipping minimal art objects, which the project's organizers could not afford anyway, they seized the opportunity to involve various people in production on site. During a shortage, workers' assistance was crucial in producing artworks. Participants of *Construction in Process* recall that the invitation came *carte blanche*, without limitations, apart from the use of hard currency, otherwise necessary expenses could be covered in kind.

The project's organizers struggled with securing provisions, and with battling food and gas shortages. Due to the recurrence of these conditions through and after the transformation period, citizens engaged in the alternative circulation of difficult-to-obtain "commodities," at least until the early 1990s. Eventually the country of constant shortages gained access to market goods, and artists entered the global art markets. In the year before Poland joined the European Union and financial help became available to address the effects of structural negligence, a Polish-Spanish artist duo created a strategic board game titled "Survivors of the White Cube."[12] The resources players could win were "budget," "time," "audience interest," and "networks."

The same year in which "Survivors of the White Cube" was launched, another Polish group took interest in commenting on the reality of global and local art markets. Four middle-aged men formed the AZORRO collective and started to document their fake "shoptalk." The videos *Everything Has Been Done part I* and *II* depict a failed brainstorming session during which members of a group try to think of something they can do as an artwork: "So, what can we do then? Yeah, exactly. Cause we have to come up with something new."[13] But apparently all the ideas they can think of have already been done, explored by someone else: "we could do nothing. But that's been done too. We have to do something because one can't do nothing anymore." The paradigm of novelty as a requirement of artists' work that AZORRO critiqued is a problem that contemporary curators also face in their work, especially individuals appointed to curate large-scale international exhibitions. The collective curating of the Kyiv Biennial in 2021 seemed to overcome that pressure by presenting the same exhibition the OFF-Biennale Budapest showed earlier in the year, titled *Transperiphery Movement: Global Eastern Europe and Global South.* Individualism, traditionally associated with taking a curatorial position, was replaced in the Alliance with a focus on facilitating local audiences' access to artworks that were treated as resources that needed to be redistributed and reused.

The curatorial collectives of the 2010s and 2020s mentioned earlier all seemed to strategize over available resources, but their approaches differ. One of the first gatherings of members of the EEBA was organized around the question of how to create "a biennale that does not end up establishing a promising career for a couple of individuals while the rest of the team is exhausted physically, mentally, and financially."[14] What could have remained a theoretical problem and a work of imagination instead became a way to reclaim collective engagement, thanks to a coalition of like-minded individuals. Forming a coalition is an exercise of solidarity in a practical sense, acting against competitions for the grants that all members rely on. A collective strategy could guarantee coherent and sustainable growth—or if not growth, then at least an existence.[15]

Considering how EEBA collectives differ from their counterparts, I would argue it is their focus on their nearest audiences. This attention for those in their direct proximity can be understood as a physical one—meaning their programs address the residents of the cities of Warsaw and Kyiv. Additionally, they treat their brand differently than biennials that use the event's location to generate its identity and attract tourism. And if the collective curating examples we've seen in Warsaw and Kyiv seem to offer a critique of individual authorship, they are arguably also a critique of the whole spectrum of problems associated with the biennialization they oppose by foregrounding the local and regional. They are also focused on benefitting communities both in and outside of the art world, as seen in The Kyiv Biennial's *School of Kyiv.*

Many in the field are familiar with exhibitionary schemes: for instance, the 7th Berlin Biennale (2012). Curated by Artur Żmijewski, who postulated it to be a "parliament rather than salon" it offered mainly disruption instead.[16] Distancing itself from mega-shows in general but also other so-called new biennials, the 7th Berlin Biennale curator invited artists commenting on current political events as well as activists, true believers in direct democracy.[17] The project was later described as eccentric due to its uncertain status and provocative attitude. Despite efforts to break with the exhibition format, the 7th Berlin Biennale was still organized as an individually visited event, whereas the Kyiv Biennial in 2015 proposed a different form of audience participation and engagement. Opening Departments of the School of Kyiv in other European cities—treating them like international branches, in Berlin, Prague, and Rome—the team organized discussions, while others undertook the organization of exhibitions focusing on Ukrainian art. The Akademie der Künste der Welt in Cologne presented *Phone Calls from the Cemetery and Other Stories*, with work by a group of Ukrainian as well as Russian artists commenting on the war in Donbass; the Badischer Kunstverein presented *Karlsruhe Class*, (lecturer: Alexandra Exter); the Museum of Contemporary Art Leipzig presented *Leipzig Class—Seminar: Politics of Form*; MUSA Vienna showed *Visiting MUSA: The School of Prosperity*, with, among others, work by Zhanna Kadyrova and Mykola Ridnyi; Kunsthall Trondheim showed *Meshes of the Afternoon— The School of Landscape: Department Trondheim*, which focused on female artists like Lada Nakonechna and Alevtina Kakhidze. In each of these cases the program was addressed at local audiences instead of art tourists. They weren't inviting visitors to travel but rather they presented work by artists based in Kyiv or associated with the city, spread out across Europe. Such large-scale collaboration was possible due to the willingness to support the Ukrainian agenda by European institutions in the period following the Euromaidan events.

A similar approach, albeit on a much smaller scale, was adopted by artist Marcin Polak, who in 2022 was invited to curate a diploma exhibition at the Art Academy in Szczecin. Polak, a member of curatorial collective Galeria Czynna (Open Gallery) and a cultural policy activist in the city of Łódź, decided not to organize students' presentation in the venue close to the Academy, only for their colleagues to see what they already knew from shared classes and studios. Instead, he co-organized a tour across Poland with pop-up student presentations addressing local art scenes and audiences.

During the second meeting of the Biennial Alliance, held in Warsaw in 2019, its members outlined the need to reconfigure the once-enforced transnational unions in the region. When confronted with some questions from the audience, EEBA members also spoke about the new neo-nationalistic political covenants as a context. One of the doubts shared by audiences concerned the scope of the Biennial Alliance's actions: "What are you really doing together?" someone asked. "And why do you use such an outdated term as Eastern Europe—are you playing it ironically?" Roughly translated, the answer was: "To tell the story of our region in our own words and regain control over the conversation."

1   On Hungarian cultural politics, see, for instance, Anita Komuves, "To Viktor, the spoils: how Orbán's Hungary launched a culture war from within," *The Calvert Journal*, September 5, 2018, available at https://www.calvertjournal.com/articles/show/10626/orban-hungary-culture-war-budapest (accessed March 9, 2023).

2   On recent Polish cultural politics, see, for instance, Magdalena Moskalewicz, "The Crisis in Poland's Museums," *Art in America*, December 17, 2021, available at https://www.artnews.com/art-in-america/columns/issues-and-commentary-zacheta-janusz-janowski-1234613869/ (accessed March 9, 2023).

3   For an overview of its initial iterations, see Hajnalka Somogyi, "Can We Work Like This? Off-Biennale Budapest," in *Curating after the Global: Roadmaps for the Present*, ed. Paul O'Neill, Simon Sheikh, Lucy Steeds, and Mick Wilson (Cambridge, MA: MIT Press, 2019).

4   Among other funds, the EEA (and Norway) Grants, the German Goethe Institut, and the Erste Stiftung act as supporters of cultural exchange in Europe. Agendas and priorities among these programs vary but their common aims are the strengthening of international relations and promotion of regional cultures.

5   It is worth noting that the Kyiv Biennial edition of 2015 was the first part of a different recurring event, titled "ARSENALE," taking place at Mystetskyi Arsenal, its main organizer. After the institution withdrew curators Hedwig Saxenhuber and Georg Schöllhammer, it managed to organize the biennial independently with the support of the Visual Culture Research Center.

6   On the legislation of historical memory in Ukraine see, for instance, Tatiana Zhurzhenko, "Legislating Historical

Memory in Post-Soviet Ukraine," in *Memory Laws and Historical Justice: The Politics of Criminalizing the Past*, ed. Elazar Barkan and Ariella Lang (London: Palgrave Macmillan, 2022).

7 Cherepanyn also spoke about the transition period of the 1990s, pointing out that it created the oligarchy and furthered inequalities.

8 The media covered a story that went viral, depicting a Ukrainian woman serving a Russian soldier entering her hometown with a handful of sunflower seeds. It was followed by a morbid comment that flowers will grow from the soil on which the soldier will die.

9 I wrote about it for a publication accompanying an exhibition at the Künstlerhaus Wien. See Christina Helbock and Dietmar Schwärzler, eds., *LOVING OTHERS—Models of Collaboration* (Vienna: Künstlerhaus Wien, 2022).

10 Which include the Kobiety Wędrowne (Nomadic Women) Foundation, the Bądź (Be) Foundation, and the Academy of Special Education.

11 See https://soniakh.com/ (accessed March 9, 2023).

12 See https://zasoby.msl.org.pl/arts/view/8264 (accessed March 9, 2023).

13 See https://zasoby.msl.org.pl/arts/view/651 (accessed March 9, 2023).

14 See the "Unlearning Biennale," October 19–20, 2018, Prague, a symposium organized by tranzit. cz with the participation of Spolek Skutek, Liverpool Biennial, Klinika, Oslo Biennial, Jakarta Biennial, Display, Casco Art Institute, Visual Culture Research Center/Kyiv Biennial, Jindřich Chalupecký Society, Biennale Warszawa, Futura Project, Berlin Biennale, Plato Ostrava,

OFF-Biennale Budapest, Nha San Collective, and ETC Gallery.

15 In February 2022, the Biennial Alliance members were forced to face Russia's full-scale aggression against Ukraine. The headquarters of the Biennale Warszawa served as a first point of contact for refugees, while the institution's online presence focused on a public program titled "The Armed Democracy: Lessons of the Russo-Ukrainian War." By decision of the mayor, the name, management, and direction were changed in September 2022. The Biennale Warszawa was formally transformed into the Warsaw Cultural Observatory, which suggests the new incarnation's aim is more passive.

16 Interestingly, the archive of the 7th Berlin Biennale was deposited by Artur Żmijewski at the Museum of Modern Art in Warsaw as an artist archive, a gesture underlining it was considered by him as an individual project, despite having previously acknowledged Joanna Warsza and the Voina collective as associate curators— presumably mainly for political effect.

17 "Contemporary art biennials, or 'new biennials', are sites of prestige, innovation and experimentation, where the category of art is meant to be in perpetual motion, rearranged and redefined, opening itself to the world and its contradictions; to the world of politics and critical theory; to the world of business and creative branding; to the world of flexible labour and urban renewal; to the world of left-wing activism and social intervention." See Panos Kompatsiaris, *The Politics of Contemporary Art Biennials: Spectacles of Critique, Theory and Art* (London: Routledge, 2017).

Information on the aims and activities of collectives and entities referenced have been derived from official statements—written and spoken—available online.

*Ja*mestown:
A Case Study on Collaborative Ethics, Developmental Curation, and the Politics of Display

Serubiri Moses

In this text, I consider several programs organized by the Foundation for Contemporary Art–Ghana (FCA Ghana), a network of artists founded as a non-profit art institution in 2004. The aim of this essay is to explore how artist collectives that follow a strategy of collaborative ethics can be understood to counter the prevalent politics of display in the Ghanaian art ecosystem. I anchor my study of the politics and ethics of the Ghanaian art ecosystem in the 1970s and 1980s structural adjustment era, the primary aim of which was to affect the development of the so-called Third World. In order to forward a properly global understanding of this ecosystem, I later refer to British-Nigerian curator Bisi Silva's notion of "developmental curation," articulated in various talks and writings, which enables an analysis of art and its development in this particular context.[1]

1970s and 1980s Structural Adjustment

If the Havana Biennial (founded in 1984) in Cuba was formed on the basis of a tricontinental economic solidarity between Africa, Asia, and Latin America, building on principles of the Non-Alignment Movement during the 1960s, then artist collectives in Senegal, South Africa, and other countries in the so-called Third World emerged in a similar context of stringent neoliberal programs, including structural adjustment in which massive amounts of debt were dispersed across said countries through the International Monetary Fund (IMF) and the World Bank. This debt dispersal coincided with the building of massive infrastructure projects funded by China and later Russia. In the post-1990s, these countries would be joined by the United States in, for example, the construction of the George W. Bush Highway in Accra, Ghana.

Historically, structural adjustment programs were implemented in periods of increased political strife, such as the military coups that took place in Ghana, Nigeria, Zaïre (later DRC), and Uganda. The subsequent military dictatorships in these countries turned flourishing art institutions into what Silva calls a "descent into mediocrity" because they led to the mass exodus of intellectuals to the US, France, Germany, and the UK. The resulting "vacuum" or "void" would later be lamented by Swiss-Cameroonian curator Koyo Kouoh as the void of the public or state-funded art institution.[2] Both Kouoh and Silva suggest that the aftermath of structural adjustment in the post-1980s called for a *tabula rasa*, a "starting from scratch," to address the decline of art infrastructure in these African nations.

In the US and UK this period brought about the rise of so-called multiculturalism, situated as a reckoning with 1960s social movements such as Black Power, the Anti-Vietnam War Movement, the Student Movement, and the Black Feminist Movement. In several exhibitions, including *The Other Story* (1989) at the Whitechapel Gallery, London, and *The Decade Show* (1989) at the New Museum, New York, Black, Latinx, Asian, Native American, women, and LGBTQ artists were ushered into the mainstream art world. It is therefore fair to say that at the time the development of the art system in the US and UK took place through the lens of "identity politics."[3] Yet one could also make the argument that the financial crisis of the 1980s in the West contributed to the resurgence of "identity politics" as demonstrated in artist groups such as Group Material, which ran a small gallery called Arroz con Mango on the Bowery in New York. Anthropologist Mahmood Mamdani has suggested that the African university became the site *par excellence* of structural adjustment programs that sought to turn the "African" institution into a commercially viable and privatized space through offering an array of short entrepreneurial courses.[4] The École des Beaux Arts at the Cheikh Anta Diop University in Dakar, Senegal, no doubt equally experienced the shocks of this economic shift.[5] In the aftermath of these developments, artists began to organize in ways that exceeded the traditional institutional framework of the École des Beaux Arts and the Museé Dynamique. The Laboratoire AGIT'Art artist collective, initiated by El Hadji Sy, Issa Samb, and Djibril Diop Mambéty, among others, was formed in Dakar amid these economic shifts in 1974. At least one advantage of the massive China-funded infrastructure initiative was that it enabled artists to occupy a construction site, which would eventually become the Village des Arts, a prominent artist studio space that still exists in Dakar today.[6] Curator and scholar Clémentine Deliss outlined the development of the Village des Arts and the context of Tenq, an artist workshop, on the disused site as follows:

> In the early 1980s, the Chinese government was commissioned by numerous West African states to design and build sports arenas in exchange for diplomatic support and trade privileges. The Chinese brought their own labourers to Senegal and built temporary housing for them in the suburbs of the city. Once the construction was completed, most of the Chinese left Senegal. Those who remained in Dakar moved out of the camp, and it remained uninhabited for over eight years. The camp had its own sophisticated system of irrigation, and a profusion of mango trees, but it was rundown and needed cleaning up. Three weeks later, in May 1996, the new Tenq, understood once again as a point of artistic connection, opened the gates of the Chinese camp to the outside world. The flimsy dividing walls in the barracks had been knocked through and studios allocated to guest artists from Kenya,

Zimbabwe, South Africa, Ivory Coast, Nigeria and
the UK, who spent two weeks living and working together
on site.[7]

Meanwhile, over the last two decades artist collectives in Ghana
have implemented subtle and effective curatorial gestures
against the backdrop of new neoliberal programs, such as those
facilitating the construction of the George W. Bush Highway in
Accra as part of the N1 Highway that connects various West
African countries by road. The resulting debt flowing into affluent
neighborhoods in Accra led artist collectives to question the
politics of display, and to form a collaborative ethic that centers the
public at large. Embracing a collaborative ethic, artists such
as Ato Annan of the Foundation for Contemporary Art–Ghana (FCA),
worked across what was seemingly a deteriorating urban space
in Jamestown, in Old Accra, the oldest part of the city. Like El Hadji
Sy and collaborators had done with the abandoned Chinese
laborer village in Dakar, together with FCA artist members and the
Accra dot Alt collective, Annan sought to occupy Jamestown in
a way that focused on what I call a "careful navigation of ownership"
within its local Ga community.

Towns Act of 1892

In 1649, the Ga king Mampong Okai granted permission
to the Dutch West India Company to build a fort and
leased land to them at Aprang, a village on the coast.
The decision infuriated the king's advisors and generals
who recalled the Portuguese presence and the cost
in lives to uproot their fort. The king would pay dearly for
giving the Dutch permission to build their lodge in Accra.
The fort was named Crevecouer [sic] but it is now called
Ussher Fort. It was renamed for a British governor Herbert
Taylor Ussher after the British bought it from the Dutch
in 1868. In 1661, Okaikoi the son of Mampong Okai
and his successor as Ga king permitted the Swedes to
begin a lodge at Osu. The Swedes were superseded
by the Dutch then the Danes who took over the fort in
the same year and built Christiansborg castle.

> The story of Jamestown began with the erection of
> James fort by the British in 1673–74. The British fort was
> the last European trading post to be erected in Accra.
> It was the smallest of the three forts and was built about
> one and half miles from the Dutch fort. It stood in a village
> called Soko owned by the Ajumaku and Adanse clans.
> The site for the fort was leased in 1672 to the Royal African
> Company by the Ga Mantse Okaikoi. King James I of
> Great Britain granted a royal charter to the company to build
> the fort and gave permission to name it after himself.[8]

This "definitive" history of Jamestown and Old Accra, by art critic
and former mayor of Accra Nat Nuno-Amarteifio, underlines the
urgent question of propriety and ownership in Ghana. Contemporary
Ghanaian law still favors land and property ownership in its
jurisdiction, which makes the idea of "public space" ambiguous.
The question is how we might better articulate this issue of ownership
as it intersects with the collaborative work carried out by artists
in what they assume to be "public" urban space, taking the form of
actions, performances, interventions, murals, and festivals.

The Towns Act of 1892 that governs Ghana's major cities,
including Accra, provides sufficient clauses for the governance of
urban spaces in the city. Sadly, it does so to the detriment of
social practice, when, for example, it states under the section titled
"Removal of Projections or Obstructions" that,

> (1) The District Chief Executive may give notice to the
> occupier or owner of a house or building to remove
> or alter a porch, shed, verandah, projecting window, step,
> pavement, sign post, show board, or any other obstruction
> or projection erected against or in front of the house or
> building which is an obstruction to the safe and convenient
> passage along the street.[9]

Bypassing this broad statute, FCA's Art in Public Space program,
initiated in 2010, took artists to unusual sites across Ghana to carry
out workshops, murals, and performances, among other projects.
It is described as extending out of another FCA program, called
Art in the Garden, which sought to provide artists with the opportunity

to show ambitious concept-driven and installation work beyond the gallery setting, and in privately owned gardens.[10] The Art in Public Space program's aims were, according to Annan, to develop a form of institutional critique that would shift the FCA's focus on private and wealthy patrons and their gated compounds, to the Jamestown public, located in one of the lower income districts of Accra.[11] The shift toward a social practice in Jamestown was therefore motivated by a class-conscious critique, likely inspired by former president of Ghana Kwame Nkrumah's own critique of postcolonial nationalism.

FCA's initial Art in Public Space program took place within a neighborhood governed by private ownership, rather than just any public place. This experience reinforced Annan's ideas developed in negotiations with Jamestown's Ga communities before the FCA's production of a mural in Akumajay Community Park in 2010.[12] As the seat of the Ga Mantse (the ruler of the Ga people, whose rule played a crucial role in the public affairs of Old Accra and Jamestown since the sixteenth century), permission to work on the mural was ultimately given by the Ga community leaders. With its few murals collectively executed by FCA artists, Art in Public Space had a seemingly modest outcome, and most commentators on recent developments in the Ghanaian art ecosystem have focused instead on the global attention and reception of Ghanaian artists in the art world.[13] Local politics, and specifically the difficulty of negotiations behind the realization of these Jamestown projects, remain largely unreported. My argument is that this is largely due to the issue of property ownership as it interfaces with collaborative ethics and what can be called "developmental curation." Annan sought permissions and carried out negotiations with the Ga chiefs in Jamestown while also seeking permissions from the Town Council of Accra.[14]

In describing the actions of FCA's Art in Public Space program, Annan used the word "happenings," a term popularized by Allan Kaprow in the mid twentieth-century US.[15] Annan emphasized the contemporary nature of the program and its attempt to give a platform for artists working in nontraditional mediums, such as video, performance, installation, and sound. This sentiment is echoed in the work of curator Silva, whose approach to art and development focused on experimental mediums and pedagogies.

Since Ghanaian law emphasizes land and property ownership, leaving almost no open or free spaces for the public as seen in metropolitan cities of the Western world, I am reminded of architect Rem Koolhaas's claim regarding the "chaos" of Lagos,[16] as well as anthropologist AbdouMaliq Simone's concept of rhythm and improvisation in Freetown, Sierra Leone.[17] While Simone offers a very different assessment from that of Koolhaas, both invite speculation on the "chaos" and/or "rhythm" of African cities. However, when the terms "chaos" and "rhythm" are used to articulate urban experiences in African cities, they can be misleading when it comes to the collective work of artists like Annan, Bernard Akoi-Jackson, or Mantse Aryeequaye. The spontaneous and improvisational nature of their public actions—such as pop-up performances and happenings, or large building-sized installations and performative processions—can be perceived as lacking rigorous engagement with the legal framework of African cities more broadly. Yet Annan and the FCA collective were conscious about their actions and engaged in proper negotiation with both the Ga chieftaincy and the community. In what could be perceived as a form of institutional critique, they turned away from the sites of Ghana's wealthy private donors toward the Ga community of Jamestown. I suggest that working within that community constitutes both an ethics of collaborative work and a careful navigation of ownership.

Collaborative Ethics and Kwame Nkrumah's Consciencism

I am interested in the move toward downtown (Old Accra) from uptown (Cantonments) as a metaphor for the radical shift in thinking that has arisen in the art ecosystem in Ghana since the mid-2000s. The move from Cantonments, an affluent neighborhood where FCA had an office, toward Jamestown, a historic district with a majority working-class public, signaled an economic and spatial shift that reminds me of the Laboratoire Agit'Art's shift to the disused Chinese village along Route de la Rufisque from the affluent (and colonial) La Plateau in Dakar. FCA's move is birthed from an internal critique, specifically driven by a class-conscious concern with the protocols of display that had become prevalent in the Ghanaian art ecosystem.[18]

   This move toward Old Accra, and the downtrodden Jamestown, was predicated on careful collaborative work with the Ga community. Given the outcomes of the collaboration—such as the mural at

Akumajay Community Park and later the development of the Chale
Wote Street Art Festival, among other projects—it is possible to
argue that this move has led to a lot of good, and not only for the
artist community in Ghana. Many installations, films, photographs,
and public projects developed in the district have led to bigger and
more lucrative opportunities, which also applies to the Ga community
in Jamestown. This includes an increase in cash flowing into the
district since 2010, where the Chale Wote Street Art Festival pulled
crowds of approximately 10,000 people in 2016 and 2017.

The move essentially embodies the formation of a collaborative
ethics that is aligned with that of philosopher and former president
of Ghana, Kwame Nkrumah's theory of cultural anthropology and his
concept of development via Consciencism. By favoring native
cultural values among the Ga community, the artist collectives recall
Nkrumah's focus on culture for development. Here, development of
the arts was enabled in the context of native culture, with Jamestown
being the location of annual festivals like Homowo and various
ritual ceremonies throughout the year, and a public beyond the
gallery-going, hotel-visiting crowd. Looking at images on the FCA
website, it is clear that artists worked together on sketches, producing
mock-ups for the murals in the old FCA Cantonments office before
going to Jamestown to produce them at Akumajay Community Park.
In addition to this collaborative approach, the images show how
the murals borrow from indigenous Ghanaian Adinkra symbols and
forms of classical African art and visual culture, if not from
a particular indigenous cosmology situated in Ghana, which only
reinforces an embrace of native culture as a tool for development.

At the core of what I referred to earlier as the "careful
navigation of ownership" is a class-consciousness that can be
found in the writings and speeches of Nkrumah. Nkrumah sought
to bring together a view of history with a critical angle from
philosophy. He elaborated his approach in the book *Consciencism*
(1970) in which he stated that, "The history of a nation is,
unfortunately, too easily written as the history of its dominant
class."[19] He challenged the idea propagated in Europe during the
Enlightenment that, "Africa was only propelled into history by
European contact,"[20] and also called out Hegel's "ahistorical"
reading of Africa as backward and lacking in progress. Ultimately,
Nkrumah challenged existing views of history and sought to provide

a class-driven historical analysis of African society, undermining the idea that Europe was at the center of Africa's development and her historical progress: "Africa cannot be validly treated merely as the space in which Europe swelled up."[21]

Nkrumah was not only an anti-racist and anti-colonial critic; he was equally interested in critiquing the upper classes and elite in Africa, which he considered as colluding with colonial structures and ideologies. His sober critique of class, made in relation to Africa's rebirth, reads as follows: "In the new African renaissance, we place great emphasis on the presentation of history. Our history needs to be written as the history of our society, not as the story of European adventures."[22] Although not spelling it out directly, this can be construed as an attack on the African middle classes and colonial subjects for whom Europe still held court on Africa's intellectual horizon. I argue that Nkrumah's ideas provide a strong basis for the curatorial strategies and interventions of artist collectives in Ghana.

In his propositions, Ato Annan challenged the exclusivity of private gardens as the domain of art for wealthy patrons, as it was practiced in FCA's Art in the Garden program. I refer to Annan's propositions as a form of institutional critique because he operated within the institutional context of FCA, even though he had not been its founder.[23] By posing the question "Does contemporary art reflect contemporary society?," the Accra conference "State of the Arts" (2004) demonstrated that the FCA was not unaware of the influence of Ghana's elite within the arts.[24] Annan et al.'s intervention engaged with the Ga community, and in doing so followed Nkrumah's plea for a focus on development rooted in culture that centered the "history of our society."

Nkrumah's concept of Consciencism and its emphasis on Ghana's cultural history as a source for development is echoed by the work of other collectives, such as blaxTARLINES, constituted of faculty and students of the KNUST Painting and Sculpture Department in Kumasi, Ghana. The collective is led by artist Bernard Akoi-Jackson, who curated the monumental exhibition *The Gown Must Go to Town* (2015), itself a citation from a speech by Nkrumah. Such collectives act within what Silva calls "developmental curation" as a way of challenging the mediocrity that plagued the art world during the post-Independence era.

Conditions of Lack

Silva has highlighted what she describes as a lack of rigorous
theoretical and critical knowledge in the university owing to
"outdated" art curricula in Nigeria.[25] In a talk at the *Creative Time
Summit* (2010) in New York, she detailed how the university
had been besieged by the regime of military dictatorship,[26] reporting
that during military rule, top intellectuals had left Nigeria for the
UK and US, leaving a university institution that therefore "descended
into mediocrity."[27] She argued for forms of creative practice that
critically respond to these conditions of lack, which also apply in the
Ghanaian art ecosystem. Such forms relate to attempts by visual
and performance artists to insert vibrant interventions in the public
sphere, using curatorial strategies to develop social practice in
the Ghanaian art context.

Whereas Silva mainly referred to the lack of public funds for
intellectual life in Nigeria, and the mass exodus of intellectuals who
had shaped these institutions, artist collectives in Ghana responded
to the elitist exclusion of the working-class publics that do not have
easy access to museums, art galleries, hotels, universities, or green
spaces. In another talk, Silva has elaborated further on what she
understands this "lack" to be.

> After living for a long time in Europe I moved back to Nigeria
> and found that even though Nigeria has a big dynamic
> visual art scene with commercial galleries, there was
> no contemporary art space that allowed for experimentation.
> Most of the exhibitions were commercial, and conservative,
> focusing on painting and sculpture, and very few platforms
> for photography, video art, performance art, sound art,
> and all these other lens-based, time-based, and experimental
> media. There were quite a few artists who did want to
> develop work and projects that engaged these media, and
> also engaged with topics that bordered on the political
> and the social. There was a lack of critical debate going on
> around the exhibitions that did take place, and (there were)
> very few libraries. The original idea was to set up a library,
> a resource center, or a research center for visual art
> and culture. However, I felt that it would be premature to

just set up a library without having a gallery space where
the exhibitions and projects could happen, and artists
as well as young art professionals who wanted to develop
a curatorial career could (have) a place or space to carry
out their curatorial activities.[28]

Silva's assessment of the cultural sphere in Nigeria mirrors my
view on the situation in Ghana: there were no spaces supporting
work other than painting and sculpture.[29] Annan and the FCA artist
collective envisioned the Art in Public Space program to provide
a platform for artists working in a variety of mediums—including
performance, installation, video, photography, and conceptual
art practices. According to Annan, the placement of the works has
resulted in an increased interest in Jamestown as a location to
experience culture.[30]

Annan was also part of the Accra dot Alt collective that founded
the Chale Wote Street Art Festival in 2011, which began a year
after the first iteration of the Art in Public Space program in 2010.
Building on the model of Art on Public Space in Jamestown, Chale
Wote's success in 2014, for example, was due to the ambitious
art installations by artists like Ibrahim Mahama, Serge Attukwei
Clottey, and Kwasi Ohene Ayeh, alongside performances by
Elizabeth Sutherland and Bernard Akoi-Jackson, all of which were
highly Instagrammable—enhancing their accessibility further.
It is worth noting that Silva repeatedly engaged with the Ghanaian
contemporary art scene through numerous visits, including
as a guest critic at the KNUST Painting and Sculpture Department.

Developmental Curation

I propose that Silva's notion of "developmental curation" and her
question "what kind of curatorial practice is possible in a context in
which infrastructural deficit, physical and intellectual, exist?" are
both generative for the Ghanaian art context.[31] If curatorial practice
is possible with little to no state support for the arts, and in a context
in which artists and cultural workers apparently do not bother
with the state either, the rise of group initiatives like FCA–Ghana,
Accra dot Alt, and blaxTARLINES can be argued to offer an
answer.[32] But first it may be helpful to consider what these initiatives

respond to. If for Silva the most pressing response was to address the intellectual vacuum at the university, what can be considered the most pressing and oppressive aspect of the Ghanaian art ecosystem?

Without a doubt military dictatorship had played a critical role, given the decades of military coups and occupation that shaped post-Independence Ghana, including the evening curfews of the 1980s. It is also clear that the artist collectives discussed so far are interested in reviving the political philosophy of Kwame Nkrumah and recasting its critical theoretical position into the realm of culture — a space that Nkrumah himself was interested in via his idea of using cultural anthropology as part of development. Either way, like Silva's CCA Lagos, these artist collectives take the approach of "developmental curation," which seeks to fill the void of a clear infrastructural deficit, particularly as it applies to the arts, while building "updated" platforms for more "conceptual" and "experimental" practices that are not that accepted yet within the country's art market and university setting. In one of their most lauded efforts, the earlier mentioned *The Gown Must Go to Town*, included ambitious projects such as Ibrahim Mahama's work covering the Kwame Nkrumah Museum of Science and Technology in jute sacks. In contrast, the Accra dot Alt collective, which between 2011 and 2016 collaborated with Annan, aimed at "transforming old Accra into a live museum," focusing on Jamestown. Chale Wote's vision was "to cultivate a wider audience for the arts in West Africa by breaking creative boundaries and using art as a viable form to rejuvenate public spaces."[33] I argue that we can view this vision through the lens of Silva's "developmental curation," given that the emphasis is on "rejuvenation" of public spaces that have become degraded or have fallen into disrepair.

One might ask to what extent rejuvenation in the Old Accra district begins to imitate the gentrification of low-income neighbor-hoods in large metropolitan cities such as Luanda and Addis Ababa. The condition of Jamestown — as the home of the Ga ruler since the sixteenth century, and a former Dutch, British, and Swedish settlement with three forts — was a core reason to develop the Chale Wote festival activities and further programming. In addition, Accra dot Alt turned the town and its main street into a "live museum," confirming the potential of developmental curation through a considered use of public space to challenge a further descent into urban blight.

1   Bisi Silva, "Regional Report," talk
    delivered at *Creative Time Summit:
    Revolutions in Public Practice*, New
    York, 2010; and Bisi Silva "Creating
    Space for One Thousand Flowers
    to Bloom," in *Àsìkò: On the Future of
    Artistic and Curatorial Pedagogies*
    (Lagos: Center for Contemporary Art
    Lagos, 2017).

2   Koyo Kouoh, "Filling the Voids:
    The Emergence of Independent
    Contemporary Art Spaces," *Condition
    Report: Symposium on Building Art
    Institutions in Africa*, ed. Koyo Kouoh
    (Ostfildern: Hatje Cantz, 2012).

3   Though it is often noted that such
    developments began in the 1960s
    with groups like the Art Workers'
    Coalition and the Black Emergency
    Cultural Coalition. See Julia Bryan
    Wilson, *Art Workers: Radical Practice
    in the Vietnam War Era* (Berkeley:
    University of California Press, 2011);
    Blake Stimson and Gregory Sholette,
    eds., *Collectivism after Modernism:
    The Art of Social Imagination after
    1945* (Minneapolis: University of
    Minnesota Press, 2007); Susan E.
    Cahan, *Mounting Frustration: The Art
    Museum in the Age of Black Power*
    (Durham, NC: Duke University Press,
    2016).

4   Mahmood Mamdani, "The African
    University," *London Review of Books*,
    July 19, 2018.

5   For an art history of the École des
    Beaux Art de Dakar led by Pierre
    Lods, see Elizabeth Harney,
    *In Senghor's Shadow: Art, Politics,
    and the Avant-garde in Senegal,
    1960–1995* (Durham, NC: Duke
    University Press, 2004).

6   Curator and scholar Elvira Dyangani
    Ose distinguished the collaborative
    work of the 1970s artist collectives
    from the national cultural policy and
    state ideology of national institutions:
    "This aesthetics began in the
    late 1970s, but only in the past two
    decades has it noticeably proliferated.
    Whereas recent scholarship
    acknowledges international events
    in the 1990s—such as DAK'ART,
    the Biennale de l'Art Africain
    Contemporain as the source of
    a significant shift in contemporary
    African art and aesthetics, I would
    propose instead that it is in local
    initiatives led by artist collectives—
    against cultural narratives and policies
    proposed by national institutions—
    that one can find the genesis for
    change and experimentation [...]
    Fundamental to this equation as well
    are the cross-cultural conversations
    of a Pan-African and African diasporic
    character taking place throughout
    the twentieth century, but which took
    on a crucial significance since late
    1960s in relation to major international
    festivals and professional encounters,
    such as the First World Festival of
    Negro Arts in Dakar, Senegal (1966),
    the First Pan-African Cultural Festival,
    PANAF, in Algiers, Algeria (1969),
    and the Second World Black and
    African Festival of Arts and Culture,
    FESTAC '77, in Lagos, Nigeria.
    A historical analysis of these events
    might provide an alternative narration
    of history that can assist us not only
    in understanding the inherent role
    of art in politics, but also in reactivating
    our political relationship to the
    practice of art in the realm of global
    politics." See Elvira Dyangani
    Ose, "For Whom Are Biennials
    Organised?," *OnCurating*, issue 32,
    ed. Nkule Mabaso, October 2016,
    available at https://www.on-curating.
    org/issue-32-reader/for-whom-
    are-biennials-organised.html#.
    ZAjKmeymMUQ (accessed March 8,
    2023).

7   Clementine Deliss, "Brothers in Arms:
    Laboratoire AGIT'Art and Tenq in
    Dakar in the 1990s," *Afterall*, no. 36,
    summer 2014, 17.

8   Nat Nuno Amarteifio, "The Definitive Story of James Town," in *Ade Sawyer*, November 10, 2015, available at https://adesawyerr.wordpress.com/2015/11/10/the-definitive-story-of-james-town-british-accra-by-nat-nuno-amarteifio/ (accessed December 7, 2022).

9   Laws of Ghana, Towns ACT, 1892, available at https://faolex.fao.org/docs/pdf/gha93491.pdf (accessed March 8, 2023).

10 "Art in Public Space," FCA Ghana, available at https://fcaghana.org/art-in-public-spaces-2/ (accessed December 17, 2022).

11 Serubiri Moses, phone interview with Ato Annan, December 17, 2022.

12 Ibid.

13 Rhoda Woets, "'Young Artists Can Try Out Everything': Redefining Contemporary Ghanaian Art in the 21st century," *Critical Interventions*, vol. 13, no. 1 (2019): 4–20.

14 Serubiri Moses, Interview with Ato Annan.

15 Ibid.

16 See Rem Koolhaas, *Lagos: How It Works* (Baden: Lars Müller Publishers, 2007).

17 See AbdouMaliq Simone, *Improvised Lives: Rhythms of Endurance in an Urban South* (Hoboken: John Wiley & Sons, 2018).

18 This means that in forming the Art in Public Space program (2010), Ato Annan was aware and critical of the supposed elitism of the FCA's Art in the Garden program (2010), which focused on wealthy patrons and their private lawns.

19 Kwame Nkrumah, *Consciencism* (New York: New York University Press, 1970), 63.

20 Ibid., 62.

21 Ibid., 63.

22 Ibid.

23 FCA was founded by a group of 20 members in circa 2004.

24 "FACING THE MIRROR: Does Contemporary Art Reflect Contemporary Society?," at State of the Arts Conference organized by Foundation for Contemporary Art Ghana, 2004, available at https://www.youtube.com/watch?v=Q4C-5N7Vb8k (accessed March 8, 2023).

25 Silva, "Regional Report"; and Silva "Creating Space for One Thousand Flowers to Bloom."

26 Silva, "Regional Report."

27 Ibid.

28 Silva, "Curating at CCA Lagos," Talk delivered online at IKT—International Association of Curators of Contemporary Art, Paris, 2013, available at https://soundcloud.com/ontheroofproject/mp3-pour-podcasting-audio (accessed December 17, 2022).

29 Serubiri Moses, Interview with Ato Annan.

30 Ibid.

31 Silva, "Regional Report."

32 Woets, "Young Artists Can Try Out Everything."

33 Abena Annan, "Chale Wote Street Art Festival 2014," *Obaasema*, July 28, 2014, available at https://obaasema.com/chale-wote-street-art-festival-2014/ (accessed March 8, 2023).

Curating Collective Infrastructures:

On the Example of Casa Gallina in Mexico City

Nina Möntmann

The title of this text can be read in two ways: as describing
a curating collective that works with infrastructures, or as outlining
a specific way of curating that is attending to or creating collective
infrastructures. In the following text I will discuss an example
that manages to merge collective curating and collective infrastructures—Casa Gallina, founded in 2013 in Mexico City.

Collective forms of organizing that do not boil down to the
primary aim of producing a static exhibition are increasingly present
in the field of art, and not only in art but also in curatorial processes.
What is striking about these developments is that collective
formations are often not limited to a team of curators or artists, but
that they connect to existing social structures, including people
and things, which may transform over time. The central concern in
many of these projects is a conscious examination of the ways
in which people are connected, how their social lives and work are

organized, and what role things and places play in these processes. In short, many of these initiatives focus on infrastructures. As a consequence, this specific form of collective curating results in generating precisely these infrastructures.

It can be argued that tying into existing infrastructures offers a possible entry point into structures of social formation such as an institution or a neighborhood. Whether these found infrastructures are official, hierarchical, and centralized, or unofficial, collective, and decentralized, determines the extent to which the curatorial can expand or improve infrastructures, or even bring about (fundamental) change from within. Irit Rogoff has spoken of efforts to "re-occupy infrastructure," which she discerns in activist projects, for instance, including in the art world or in the work of NGOs.[1] documenta 15, with its *lumbung* concept and the collaboration of more than 1,500 artists, most of them working in collectives, could certainly be described as a best practice model of reoccupying infrastructures, or rather, as a collective approach to curating infrastructures on a large scale.[2] While this temporary large-scale platform is gaining exorbitant public attention due to it being regarded as the most important exhibition of the international contemporary art world, there are other, more hidden, long-term, local, and situated projects that collectively develop —with a nod to Donna Haraway's idea of "situated knowledges"— the activation of partial and context-specific perspectives.

The outstanding example that I will discuss in the following emerged in 2013, when Osvaldo Sanchez, then artistic director of inSite, a binational festival of visual art in Tijuana, Mexico, and San Diego, California, took the radical step of abandoning the spectacle of a festival format in favor of establishing a more discreet local and collective initiative, Casa Gallina in Mexico City.[3] The decision to combine the resources of an international festival with a focus on public, socially committed art, in a longer-term local project signals an interest in discovering potential for the future—one that prioritizes the sustained cooperation with a local public, in the collaborating institution's structures, and collective curatorial, artistic, and organizational working processes.

The fact that no curatorial statement was published before the project got underway placed the emphasis clearly on the process of collaborating with the inhabitants of the barrio, on their interests, needs, and willingness to participate. Communication with local residents soon led to the identification of topics and serious problems that shape their everyday lives and on which the activities of Casa Gallina would focus, which were: a lack of trust between people, loneliness, a lack of resources, neglected public infrastructures, and the poor economic situation of local businesses.

The Barrio

At first glance, Santa María La Ribera seems to have all the qualities that encourage gentrification: proximity to the city center; a lively market; the shady Almeda Park with the Morisco kiosk that hosts various cultural activities; the popular Geological Museum with which Casa Gallina collaborates on many educational and artistic projects; the Chopo University Museum with its glass and iron Art Nouveau architecture; many restaurants and cafés; and a certain amount of older buildings. As shown in *Mapeo Collectivo* by the Argentinian collective Iconoclasistas, an early project at Casa Gallina, processes of gentrification have been noticeable in the barrio since the mid-1990s.[4] In their map, Iconoclasistas highlight indicators such as speculation with residential and commercial real estate. During their residency at Casa Gallina in 2015, they worked with local residents to create the map with a focus on factors that directly influence quality of life in the neighborhood: infrastructure such as public transport; green spaces; food shops and the market; the state of the roads; the state of the buildings; the development of the real estate market; and the use of public space. The obvious dilapidation of many buildings, as well as the abundance of unattractive, run-down, box-like units that were erected quickly as social housing after the 1985 earthquake, may partly explain why gentrification has yet to make itself more strongly felt. Although the area has become more attractive in recent years, the atmosphere of a quiet, green neighborhood is deceptive. The barrio still has problems with safety, violence, and waste disposal, problems Mexico's government does not seem to be able get under control.

  The barrio is home to low-income families, many impoverished pensioners, and a small number of middle-class people. There are many family-run restaurants and other small businesses. The Casa Gallina team communicates with the neighbors in the barrio primarily via Facebook and other social media. Luis Gomez, who also looks after the Casa Gallina website and the archiving of photographic documentation after every event, sits at his computer in the library and checks whether all the friend requests from neighbors really do come from the barrio. To make sure the Facebook platform remains a safe space for exchange between neighbors, he does not accept requests from outside the barrio or from members of the art world.

The Building

The nucleus of Casa Gallina is its building, the physical space of the Casa and its garden. The immediate impression on entering the garden courtyard, with its bright warm colors and its chickens and spaces opening up from it, is that of an inviting oasis of peace and quiet, a refuge.

All that can be seen on the inconspicuous façade is a small flag with a Russian-doll-style image of a chicken in an egg in a chicken in an egg, etc., and the words "Salón Huev@." From the street, then, Casa Gallina cannot be identified, as it is not marked as a public place, and certainly not as an art institution. Rather it is situated as a space shielded from the art world and from passers-by, reserved for specific activities and accessible to inhabitants of the barrio on the condition of active engagement. In this spirit, no press release was published to mark the foundation of Casa Gallina and no news is passed on to the art press. These rules of access, constantly evolving in discussion between the team and local residents, not only allow the people of the barrio to help shape what Casa Gallina is and does, but also ensure the opacity needed to try out a new quasi-institutional model of social innovation and allow socially committed art projects to operate without being immediately usurped by the art scene.[5]

The specific use of the rooms is reflected in details that have a key impact: the library is enlivened with several freely usable computers, and many books and magazines are in use, have bookmarks, and lie around in piles. The knowledge that resides in the correspondingly named zone of the house, "Saberes/Knowledges," appears to be lived knowledge, be it of the neighbor who sits at one of the computers almost daily, conducting research, or the communication and exchange between the groups of children who meet regularly with supervisors to do their homework. Project groups on various courses sit in the meeting rooms, those attending the neighborhood dinners sit in the kitchen and on the terrace, neighbors borrow tools, household appliances, and other utilitarian objects from the *Prestaduría Vecinal* (Neighborhood Lending Program), while those taking part in art projects meet at the Casa for discussions before setting off for research at other places in the barrio. The garden at the back of the site has been cultivated during Urban Farm Advanced Group Sessions, while the "Salon Huev@," with its participatory film program has established itself as a weekly meeting place for film fans; it is the only room at the Casa to be temporarily opened onto the street during the screenings.

Instead of an underlying curatorial concept, a functional layout was planned for the building, dividing it into zones: "Knowledges" is the space that holds the library, computers, and meetings. Together with the kitchen, it forms the core of the Casa. Moving around the building, one necessarily passes through this brightly lit, open space. In this way, encounters between people, collective learning, and the sharing and exchanging of knowledge are already inscribed on the level of the physical space. Leaving the "Knowledges" zone, one automatically enters the kitchen, opening onto the terrace with a big table and the garden beyond. The kitchen is where the weekly neighborhood suppers take place for which people register in advance and are put together in cross-generational groups. As well as being the venue for the "Kitchen Lessons"—workshops on cooking and nutrition—it is also where the team eats together every day, where birthdays are celebrated, and where every new visitor is welcomed with a cup of coffee. Neighbors who visit regularly may also use the kitchen. As the base of the building, the physical rooms on the ground floor contain a range of social spaces, connected by infrastructures that reflect the values and parameters of the Casa's experimental activities in the neighborhood—trust, micro-economy, belonging and communication, solidarity, local action, preservation of the environment and one's own body.

Alternative Infrastructures

A unique quality of Casa Gallina is that it operates three (sometimes interlocking) activities or collective curatorial strategies in parallel. The "Synergies" platform brings together projects organized by the team that are often carried out in collaboration with other barrio-based organizations or experts. The "Knowledges" platform aims to "promote and distribute shared knowledge and topics of interest to the community. The courses and workshops, events and activities in spaces and/or local areas are focused on making an impact on the economic and social condition of the group." And finally, "Artist Commissions" are participatory projects by artists who, if they are not from Mexico City, stay at the Casa for a residency which lasts between several months and a year.

One objective of the "Synergies" platform is to "promote local economies in a spirit of mutual collaboration, support and solidarity in existing family businesses located in the barrio or to add quality or expertise to services and businesses. Thus, this platform seeks to energize the neighborhood's social life and its efficiency and benefits." In this spirit, after it became clear from conversations with neighbors that the many family restaurants in the barrio often operated under poor economic conditions, the Casa invited the renowned chef and restaurant consultant Ivan Icra Salicru to assess their challenges and offer his expertise. As well as insufficient business planning, Salicru identified skewed social relations, such as widespread mistrust toward neighboring restaurant owners, as a cause of these economic disadvantages. He suggested reducing the size of menus, even if nearby restaurants were offering more dishes, and bulk-ordering ingredients together with other restaurants to reduce costs. Step by step, the message was conveyed that cooperation is better for everyone and rivalry is ultimately bad for the majority. Rivalry as a symptom of the neoliberalism that has brought major changes to local economic conditions in Mexico since the 1990s was already highlighted by Michel Foucault when he wrote that the neoliberal order is "not so much [about] the exchange of commodities as the mechanisms of competition."[6]

Examples from the "Knowledges" platform, supervised by education curator David Hernández and artist Rodrigo Simancas Mercado, include computer courses for older people, research projects and publications, and the Open Kitchen and Urban Farm workshops. Knowledge is treated here as non-hierarchically shared research and practice, and as relevant to the improvement of coexistence and economic conditions in the barrio. The events and the information center at the Casa therefore focus "on sustainability, architecture and urban planning, housing, city and territory, popular culture, urban visibility, food, sociology and defense of leisure."

I refer to the function of the Casa as an "alternative infrastructure" because, as Rogoff has correctly pointed out, the infrastructures widely praised in our time (especially in the West), such as "functioning institutions, systems of classification and categorization, archives and traditions […] funding and educational pathways, excellence criteria […] and properly air conditioned auditoria" may be achievements that regulate our coexistence and facilitate working processes. However, they also "become protocols that bind and confine us in their demand to be conserved or in their demand to be resisted."[7] In the current period of political upheaval, Rogoff argues, key functioning infrastructures should be preserved, while establishing spaces that foster opportunities to participate in shaping social change. Such access is provided above all by projects that operate on a local level. This re-occupying of infrastructure also implies a calling into question of the dominant infrastructures that reproduce Western values. By contrast, alternative infrastructures respond flexibly to specific local contexts and permit informal approaches and organizational processes that allow a maximum of participation. Within the Casa's alternative infrastructure, management is largely integrated into programming processes, following the same logic: teamwork is non-hierarchical and there are no assistants; one-third of the team comes from the barrio and as many services as possible are sourced in the neighborhood so as to use and support the local economy. Here again, the building is activated as a nexus in an expanding and many-layered local network.

One example of an attempt to build trust in the neighborhood is the abovementioned *Prestaduría Vecinal*, which opens three times a week for local residents to borrow tools. Without leaving a deposit or showing ID, the tools are lent out on the basis of trust. And this really works, with all tools having been returned to date. This means that relying on trust—the lack of which is a problem in the neighborhood—an operation was launched that can serve as a model for other local sharing programs and cooperations. The experiences with the *Prestaduría Vecinal* may have an educational impact that could improve coexistence in the barrio in the longer term. The example of the *Prestaduría Vecinal* shows that a unique absence of institutional categories—such as the focus on objects, the distinction between exhibition and educational program, safety regulations, the need to insure works on loan, the need to maximize visitor numbers and deliver a profit—allows Casa Gallina to develop as a platform for civil society that can operate with an alternative infrastructure and without the pressure of running art projects within the framework of an exhibition.

The Role of the Art Projects

In view of the situation in the barrio, and in the context of the "Synergies" and "Knowledges" platforms, it is no surprise that many of the art projects at Casa Gallina deal with communication and with the body as a resource. Problems frequently raised in the barrio, as in other neighborhoods inhabited by the lowest income working classes, are the lack of education, of economic resources, and of social networks.

There are many intersections between the art projects and the themes of the Casa's "Knowledges" and "Synergies" platforms: on environmental issues, for example, or support for communications between the people of the barrio. Edith Medina, a pioneer of "BioArt" in Mexico, worked with a group of teenagers in the covered market where they collect organic waste and turn it into biomaterial. Over a period of many months, the artist Marianna Dellekamp met regularly with a group of women aged between sixteen and eighty-two with a shared interest in knitting. Through the personal objects that the participants were asked to bring to the meetings, she stimulated conversations about their life stories. Dellekamp herself says that the activities in her projects are just an occasion for communication and that as activities they are interchangeable.[8] What matters is the group dynamics that take shape around these activities. Dellekamp reported that in contrast to earlier participatory projects she did, Casa Gallina's collective infrastructures offered a safe space for the participants, who were always warmly welcomed and given support by the team. In this way, the project developed a particular intimacy on the basis of which lasting contacts were established between neighbors. In the sustained processes during which a relationship with participants is built up over many months, the personality of the artists in question is put to the test, tending to play a greater role than it does in other projects. Dellekamp, for example, offered a group of people of very different ages a routine and structure that suited them all, and other artists showed great patience in building trust over long periods and conveying not only their expertise but also their own curiosity, thus creating a safe space for participants to channel their fascinations and passions into the project, but also their concerns and anxieties.

Conclusion

The collective alternative infrastructures set up by the initiative at Casa Gallina and reaching out into the barrio have been a key factor contributing to the project's success. The importance of infrastructures for long-term initiatives is huge, since "infrastructure emerges as the invisible force of manifest culture today: subversive possibilities of working with infrastructures as sites of affect and contradiction."[9] In order to bring about change in society—even in a limited local setting—it is necessary to uncover subversive potential, redefine infrastructures, and redraw the map of their functions. To summarize: Casa Gallina uses a form of "critical management" that does not follow the politics of art institutions shaped by neoliberal constraints. The hierarchies within its team are flat, everyone enters into contact with the neighbors in the barrio to an equal extent; a festival budget is used, but without submitting to the economy of obligatory visibility; at least one-third of team members are from the barrio and as many services as possible are sourced in the neighborhood; ethical principles like trust form the basis of projects like the *Prestaduría Vecinal*. At the same time, the specific design and usage of the building is not only meaningful in terms of practicality and hospitality, but it also favors the flow of these new infrastructures.

Casa Gallina can be viewed as an experiment in social innovation that can act as a model for both socially committed art and for the creation of collective infrastructures in public institutions. Casa Gallina operates in the local milieu of a neighborhood in Mexico City and has neither the range nor the ambition to generate direct change, but it does demonstrate mechanisms by which participatory processes and alternative infrastructures can inform broader contexts of political democratization. If one also takes into consideration the relative weakness of civil society in Mexico, this represents a huge step achieved by a leap of faith in local people. The mechanisms of art are transferred, in parallel and in connection with educational projects, into people's everyday lives, where they strengthen civic commitment and open up long-term prospects of participation in society. In this context, curating collective infrastructures at the Casa acts as a "medium" whose functions can be described using a definition proposed by Keller Easterling as "interlocking ecologies of effects, affects, protocols, groups, individuals and so on."[10] For this work that spans different fields, the Casa's curating of collective infrastructures is fundamental. It enables the emergence of precisely these functions as interlocking ecologies in a new combination, creating a resonant chamber for collective civic engagement, participatory commitment built on trust, and public art in equal measure.

1   Irit Rogoff, "Keynote Lecture: Infrastructure," March 20, 2013, *Former West.org*, available at https://formerwest.org/ DocumentsConstellationsProspects/ Contributions/Infrastructure (accessed March 8, 2023).

2   "Lumbung" refers to an Indonesian rice barn, in which any surplus harvest is stored and then distributed as determined collectively by the community.

3   See https://casagallina.org.mx/en (accessed March 8, 2023.

4   Communicator Julia Risler and graphic artist Pablo Ares have been working together under the name Iconoclasistas since 2006, realizing collective projects to strengthen the cohesion and collaborative resources of communities.

5   On strategic opacity in the art world, see Nina Möntmann, "Opacity," in *Abstraction*, ed. Maria Lind (London/ Cambridge, MA: Whitechapel Gallery/ MIT Press, 2013), 182–85.

6   Michel Foucault, *The Birth of Bio-politics* (New York: Picador–Palgrave Macmillan, 2008 [1978–79]), 147.

7   Irit Rogoff, "Infrastructure," in *Former West: Documents, Constellations, Projects* (Berlin: Haus der Kulturen der Welt, 2013), 31.

8   In conversation with the author on April 5, 2018.

9   As formulated in the announcement of the Bergen Assembly 2016, curated by freethought, on the notion of infrastructure.

10 Keller Easterling, *Medium Design* (Moscow: Strelka Press, 2017), unpaginated.

This text includes reworked excerpts from a previous publication: Nina Möntmann, "Withdrawal into the Public Sphere: Casa Gallina as a Model of Hospitality and Alternative Infrastructures," in Experiences of a Common Good/inSite Casa Gallina, *ed. Pablo Lafuente (México City: Casa Gallina, 2018), 233–48.*

Breaking Bad at documenta 15:

Collective Curatorial Resistance and the Case for and against ruangrupa

Gregory Sholette

Between early January and the end of September 2022, the art world was delivered a grand, and some would say disquieting or even tragically failed experiment in decentralized collective curating, pivoting on the work of largely marginal and excluded practitioners.[1] Almost from the start, this risky cultural venture became cemented within a deepening well of controversies. Labeled as offensive, scandalous, antagonistic, chaotic, artistically bad, and above all antisemitic, what documenta 15 brought to my mind instead was Lucy R. Lippard's well-known comparison between activist art and the fabled Trojan Horse. Lippard describes the dual function of this mythical "poison gift" as simultaneously a "subversion on the one hand and empowerment on the other."[2] Activist art operates, she continues, both within and "beyond the beleaguered fortress that is high culture or the 'art world.'" documenta 15 could therefore be envisioned as the clever breaching of a storied institution by a peripheral army of *others*—perhaps with some spectral assistance from Joseph Beuys of documenta 5, and Okwui Enwezor's documenta 11. By first entering, and then proceeding to throw wide open the doors of Germany's premier curatorial project, the curators of documenta 15 stirred the institution to close ranks against them in an effort to distance their project from the established German art scene. The pitched cultural battles that emerged around documenta 15 will forever mark 2022 as a decisive year for potential art world transformation, or antithetically, for its retrenchment. Either way, documenta 15 leaves the field of contemporary high culture rattled, wounded, indignant, and even retaliatory.

———

Noted for over six decades of challenging and highly intellectual contemporary art programming, documenta is centered in Kassel, Germany, a normally quiet, middle-class city of primarily German nationals, a substantial number of whom are over 60 years of age, although younger immigrants from Africa, Turkey, and other parts of Asia increasingly make up a growing percentage of the population.[3] For exactly one hundred days every five years this unremarkable place is transformed into a bingeable art festival, drawing thousands of international art world aficionados who are eager to be startled, delighted, and sometimes outraged by innovative exhibitions and installations that are spread about the city's walkable expanse. documenta has a particular distinction that it allows its selected curator(s) to take a degree of risk not possible in the Venice Biennale or other global art phenomena of similar scale. Risk is, or has been, the signature feature of documenta's various iterations, as exemplified in 2002, when the late Nigerian-born poet and curator Okwui Enwezor was selected to direct documenta 11. Although the exhibition was ultimately more conventional than many anticipated, Enwezor managed to introduce into the project what was then a startling idea, namely that the "avant-garde had never belonged to the North Atlantic alone."[4]

Enwezor, together with six co-curators,[5] accomplished his challenge to conventional curating by extending the concept of the documenta 11 program far beyond Kassel as well as Germany, with the core exhibition conjoined by satellite projects in other, external locations, including Lagos, Nigeria; Johannesburg, South Africa; New Delhi, India; and St. Lucia in the Caribbean. Rather than offer traditional exhibitions, these ancillary "Platforms" consisted of discursive events featuring philosophers, scholars, and political activists conversing on such non-art centered concerns as Democracy, Creolization, Cities Under Siege, and Truth and Justice—all focusing on conflicted relations between the Northern Hemisphere and the so-called Global South.

Twenty years later, the Indonesian art collective ruangrupa radically expanded Enwezor's partial breach of documenta's Eurocentric façade. Not only did ruangrupa itself hail from the Global South, the group explicitly embraced a collaborative ethos while neither being an NGO nor another formal type of institution. Instead, the curator of the 2022 documenta 15 was an informally structured aggregate of ten people, including several members with non-art world credentials—a journalist, ecologist, and an academic. More disconcerting still, ruangrupa completely circumvented the usual display of earnest if familiar institutional critique artists by attempting to make concrete the variety of socially engaged, mostly collectivized visual culture that thrives well beyond high art's white cube citadels. What, then, was the focus of documenta 15 in Kassel? According to ruangrupa it was "Humor, Independence, Generosity, Transparency, Sufficiency, and Regeneration," adding that "the core values and ideas of *lumbung* [an Indonesian term for a communal rice barn] as an artistic and economic model is rooted in principles such as collectivity, communal resource sharing, and equal allocation, and is embodied in all parts of the collaboration and the exhibition."[6]

ruangrupa's approach to the project intentionally decentralized their own curatorial authority by inviting a cluster of fourteen other art collectives, which in turn invited still more artists and collectives and literally brought the total number of participants close to or beyond 1,000 individuals. The exact number is difficult to calculate given the fluid nature of many groups, a point I will return to below. While it is true that Enwezor challenged documenta's standard authorial approach by inviting other curators to collaborate with him in 2002, and other iterations followed his example subsequently,[7] one could say that ruangrupa raised this proposition to full volume with their theoretically endlessly branching organizing strategy. When considered together with their non-Western geographical status it appears the Indonesian faction set out to first appropriate, and then perversely upcycle documenta's very structure into a vehicle for collective social and aesthetic experiences. Inevitably, this also infected the famed project's cultural status, its commercial utility to Kassel, and even its typically unspoken "Germanness."

A controversial outcome of one type or another was entirely predictable given the risks that ruangrupa took by opening up the curatorial process so dramatically. Could it have been otherwise? As the German philosopher of cynical (some would say curmudgeonly) reason, Peter Sloterdijk stated, "we are observing the mobilization of a post-colonial intellectual culture," adding that "Intellectuals from the periphery [are prepared to] take power in the center."[8] We might rephrase his comments more directly this way: Dear elite, what on bloody earth did you expect to happen when you handed-over this prestigious exhibition to a pack of resentful outliers?

It would be fair to suggest that ruangrupa's ethno-political and collectivist methodology struck the professional art establishment as a militant assault on entitled Western, white culture, perhaps somewhat akin to the wave of global monumenticides that followed the brutal police murder of George Floyd in 2020—although a better comparison is with Occupy Wall Street, which I will expand on later. But it would also be facile to stop there in order to avoid the risk of playing into the thinly disguised xenophobic narratives such as "[ruangrupa] is probably better seen as an agitprop outfit which seized the opportunity to use the largesse provided by the German authorities to propagate its political outlook"[9]; or more subtle expressions of repulsion including, "those responsible for the documenta must now live up to their social responsibility and draw the necessary conclusions"[10]; as well as genuine awe, "this level of autonomy felt riotous and profuse, like vegetation in an Amazonian jungle."[11] Regardless, for too many in the mainstream media and art press, this awe soon morphed to vehemence and then into outright hostility, ultimately going far beyond accusations of bigotry, to become itself a chorus of intolerance and Eurocentric chauvinism, before giving birth, all too predictably, to an apparatus of partial censorship. This is likely due to ruangrupa's socially minded and anti-market approach, which was assuredly raising a host of questions about the very nature of high art today.

———

"There will be consequences," Walter White of the TV series *Breaking Bad* ominously stated, as if anticipating a profusion of proclamations attacking documenta 15, such as *Der Spiegel*'s indignant declaration that, "the German cultural sector has a big problem."[12] Certainly, the very institution that is documenta has its own historical repetitions to deal with, including the recurring wound of Germany's twentieth-century war crimes and genocide that has hovered over the project from the start, when Werner Haftmann, a former member of the Nazi Party's paramilitary SA (Storm Troopers) initially founded the Kassel-based project in 1955.[13] Haftmann's background only came to light in 2021, the year in which ruangrupa was busily preparing for their debut on that stage, and incredibly, the timing of this discovery has been cited by some as background to their project's own alleged antisemitism.[14]

To be sure, there are outstanding issues to be addressed regarding documenta 15, especially a set of two-decades-old, pernicious caricatures of Israeli military men depicted with long-established anti-Jewish features. Discovered just five days after its public opening, the odious depictions were tucked in among hundreds of tightly packed, frequently exaggerated, and often parodic drawings making up an enormous free-standing canvas mural entitled *People's Justice.* Making matters worse, *People's Justice* was centrally located just outside the Fridericianum, which serves as documenta's cardinal reference point for some over half a million attending visitors during recent editions. Three days later, the group issued what appears to be a sincere and reflective apology denouncing racism in all forms and acknowledging the particular circumstances of documenta itself, apologizing to "all viewers and the team of documenta 15, the public in Germany and especially the Jewish community. We have learned from our mistake, and recognize now that our imagery has taken on a specific meaning in the historic context of Germany."[15]

But one month later, another set of antisemitic images targeting Israeli soldiers occupying Palestinian land ignited the press, this time found in a replica of a 1988 brochure displayed by the independent research project known as Archives of Women's Struggles in Algeria (*Archives des luttes des femmes en Algérie*). While I visited documenta 15 in June, I did not see or notice this image, but I did come across other archival publications from the early twentieth century that displayed overtly racist depictions of African and African American people performing the "Cakewalk," an arguably similarly offensive historical portrayal that, as far as I know, went entirely uncommented upon by the media.

While all of these images are harmful, isn't it the very nature of an archive to consist of precisely what it actually contains? After all, this is the key difference between the archive and historical narratives, which, as Walter Benjamin hauntingly observed, are always written by the victor, as opposed to the defeated.[16] These sordid discoveries preceded artist Hito Steyerl's unsettling withdrawal of her artwork in early July. As one of the only German citizens participating in documenta 15, and also a highly prominent mixed-race practitioner, Steyerl's vanishing act based on her lack of "faith in the organization's ability to mediate and translate complexity," along with that of Meron Mendel, a Jewish academic advisor employed to uncover any remaining transgressive imagery, appears to have spurred the resignation of documenta director Sabine Schormann one month later. For his part, Mendel clearly grasped the complexity of views involved at the time, including recognizing the cultural and political identification that members of the Global South might harbor toward people of color undergoing apartheid-like conditions in Israel (my phrase not his). But then, with a drastic and final punishing pronouncement he exited after stating that "the documenta is in ruins."[17] Still other, less nuanced voices of the German press condemned Shormann for violating "her duty of supervision," adding that therefore her resignation had nothing to do with capping the freedom of art, but "with the circumstance of protecting the boundaries of what art is."[18] Significantly, the same journalist previously condemned ruangrupa not for antisemitism, but for having gathered together in Northern Hesse a tribelike, polyphonic choir of "the angry, the disenfranchised (of every kind), the diverse (also "neurodiverse"), the marginalized, the colonized of this world.[19]

While Steyerl has added nothing further to her protest action since documenta ended in late September, there was a hush of silence by the mainstream German press toward a remarkably supportive, pro-documenta 15 communiqué from the collective Casa do Povo (The People's House) in late July. The Brazilian-Jewish cultural center had previously been considered for official invitation by ruangrupa but was then passed over. And yet, Casa do Povo insisted on full advocacy for rugangrupa's "unique, decentralized community of artists, friends," stating that,

> we have admired the way the artistic team decided to work: the idea of turning documenta into an open resource for so many collectives and artists is fascinating. Of course, the decentralization of decision-making can imply a partial loss of control. So we knew that problems could come up but we also hoped that these issues could be dealt with collectively.[20]

It is possible to argue that documenta 15's scandal boils down to several luckless missteps by the organizing collective, but still, wasn't it precisely ruangrupa's overt display of collective and rhizomatic organizing that both led to the crisis and that also came under attack from the very start? Consider the previously cited comments regarding the display of resentment by angry, colonial subjects, but also these headlines by numerous media sources such as:

> "Documenta 15's focus on Populist Art Opens the Door to Art Worlds You Don't Otherwise See–and May Not Always Want to" (Ben Davis, *Artnet.com*, July 6)

> "Friendship and Antagonism: Documenta 15" (Minh Nguyen, *Art in America*, August 2)

> "The DIY Chaos of Documenta" (Nadine Khalil, *Frieze*, July 7)

> "Documenta 15 is a Global-South-Centric Event. But Who is its Intended Audience?" (Mary Corrigall, *Latitudes* [South Africa], July 13)

And those after the antisemitic imagery was exposed in the media:

> "Documenta Was a Whole Vibe. Then a Scandal Killed the Buzz" (Siddhartha Mitter, *New York Times,* July 5)

"Documenta Art Fair Turned Ugly by Antisemitism and
Agitprop" (Leonid Bershidsky, *The Washington Post*,
July 21)

"German Jewish community wants 'consequences' for
anti-Semitic art at Documenta 15 festival" (Orit Arfa,
Israel Hayom newsletter, July 22)

"Documenta will now come under greater government
control…" (Kabir Jhala, *The Art Newspaper*, June 28)

———

Crucially, it is important to note that angry threats, and even
vandalism toward documenta 15 began well before the objectionable
imagery was ever detected and removed in mid-June. As early as
January, the Palestinian collective The Question of Funding, was
anonymously assailed online by the Alliance Against Anti-Semitism
Kassel blog, over links between the group and the Boycott, Divestment,
and Sanction (BDS) human rights campaign, following the German
Bund (parliament) branding BDS antisemitic in 2019.[21] This online
ambush was followed by a physical attack on the group's installation
in Kassel in May that included what could be read as coded threats of
future violence against the collective and its members.[22]

   If we are willing to consider the possibility that ruangrupa and
their guests were already earmarked for a particularly type
of political denunciation, which was quite unlike the effects of the
negative financial assessment that plagued Adam Szymczyk et al.'s
documenta 14 in 2017, then this reprimand could only stem from
a rejection of the group's collective, rhizomatic approach overall, that
is to say, its soft form of cultural politics. In this sense, ruangrupa's
offense was to have initiated a soft occupation of the institution
known as documenta, including engaging in a tactical disregard for
normative discerning, juridical, hegemonic forms of curating. In
fact, ruangrupa's "bad curating" resembled their own communal art
practice back in Indonesia. According to Carlos Garrido Castellano
writing about the group in 2020, its foundation involved being
flexible in its structure whereby, "ruangrupa relies on spontaneous
collaboration with colleagues and 'creators' from all around Java,

including DJs, music bands, comic producers, performance artists or graphic designers." Castellano raises some key questions, asking "how can we aesthetically evaluate their [ruangrupa's] action, when this action consists in articulating bonds with other collaborative groups with differentiated aesthetic values and strategical objectives?" and then adds, "what happens when collective initiatives such as ruangrupa acquire the size and the features of alternative art institutions?"[23] He further speculates that ruangrupa's exuberant communality that goes far beyond the "art world" does *not,*

> imply political or social disinterest, rather it reveals the extent to which collective experimentation, the precariousness of cultural labor and broader class and social concerns, are intertwined in ruangrupa's activity. And although some elements of that activity are directed toward negative aspects of the Indonesian and global society, this criticism is channeled through an accumulative, affirmative logic.[24]

In other words, what if documenta 15's seemingly playful nonchalance concerning proper institutional selectivity and curatorial restraint was itself the collective's logical adaptation to specific material and historical circumstances? A type of contemporary politics? Here I cannot help but think of the swarm-collective that was Occupy Wall Street (OWS), and how it refused to provide the media, the public, or the New York police with a list of demands for ending their intervention of Zuccotti Park in 2011. Instead, the occupation was its own alternative universe.[25] You either accepted its largely self-contained act of world-building, flaws and all, or you did not. Nobody inside the encampment really seemed to care what you thought—although similar occupations of urban plazas and parks quickly spread, spore-like, to other national and international cities, just as OWS itself was awoken by public interventions taking place across the Middle East and Madrid. Likewise, any attempts at negotiating or imposing new regulations could not withstand the occupiers' simple refrain to either join us or ignore us, to either enter into their wild 99% corral, or just walk past it. It took an early-morning police assault in mid-November, combined with the trashing of the "People's Library," and a phalanx of power-wash pavement scrubbers to finally erase OWS from

Manhattan's urban terrain, although not from the phantom archive of cultural activism: that fragmented surplus storehouse of collective imaginaries involving hopes and failures, obstinacy and resistance, joyful embarkations and unpredictable endings.[26]

Consequently, while a true measure of autonomy was present throughout all documenta 15 group projects, to the point of stirring up unsupervised and unwanted controversies and disputes, this autonomy also provided participating artists a degree of detachment from expectations about the normative task of aesthetically pleasing their audience. Still, one ambition that was consistently on display throughout the hundred days was a particular type of resolution-oriented critical pedagogy that offered a strong contrast to the familiar form of institutional critique, which was simultaneously on display at the Berlin Biennale some 235 miles away, to which I will return. Again, the Palestinian group The Question of Funding serves as a good example of this instructional intent, and their project *Dayra* also serves to reiterate key aspects of ruangrupa's overarching *lumbung* approach as presented in their mission statement, "ruangrupa invites community-oriented collectives, organizations, and institutions from around the world to practice *lumbung* with each other and work on new models of sustainability and collective practices of sharing."[27]

According to the group's website, *Dayra* is an "Arabic word meaning circle and circulating, it is a noun and a verb, where the act of sharing, and moving local resources helps the community to maintain its wealth."[28] The project consisted of a digital media installation (not damaged in the earlier anti-Islamic attack on the group's work) invoking what geographer Katherine Gibson describes as a post-capitalist community economy consisting of, "ethical economic practices that acknowledge and act on the interdependence of all life forms, human and nonhuman."[29] In a sequential graphic animation *Dayra* walks viewers through the process of arriving at a sustainable model for cultural production, one that the group has been exploring in relation to the problematic situation of Palestinian artists in the occupied territories controlled by Israel. The aim of this experiment is to wean the Palestinian cultural community off its dependency on support from external NGOs in three phases: first by questioning and debating the shortcomings of this situation; then by exploring communal blockchain-driven economic platforms;

and finally by basing these efforts at gaining greater autonomy on a trust verses zero trust system of exchange and community-building.

According to one member, The Question of Funding is "not about institutional critique; we already know it." Instead "the question is: how do we practice it? And how do we practice it outside of the art world?"[30] Likewise, the project *Dayra* did not simply bypass social and institutional analysis, but extended this criticism to problem-solving via actual, implementable action. *Dayra*'s focus, therefore, on viable alternatives to the finance and debt trap of global philanthropy, reflects documenta 15 as a whole and we can now see how ruangrupa's project diverged from many other contemporary curatorial projects, including the Berlin Biennale which I will discuss in the following section.

———

Curated by the gifted Algerian-French artist Kader Attia, the Berlin Biennale offered many excellent works of critical art, even if its general approach was a familiar one hinging on an academically informed critique of neoliberal capitalism, hetero-patriarchy, xenophobia, and colonialism. At best richly informational, at worst leadenly didactic, the Berlin exhibition was not without its own controversies, including the withdrawal of work by three Iraqi artists protesting an installation displaying Abu Ghraib prison-torture photographs from circa 2003. Among other works, the 2022 Berlin exhibition offered viewers a clever and timely investigative work on recent Russian missile strikes in Ukraine as analyzed by the collective Forensic Architecture. Maithu Bùi's vertiginous augmented-reality projection sought to exorcize historical amnesia about the role of Western colonialism in Southeast Asia. Ariella Aïsha Azoulay's epic timeline of weaponized rape established itself as a massive dossier of revisionist history focusing on the allied occupation of Berlin in the late 1940s. Lawrence Abu Hamdan offered a stunning data visualization of the Israeli army's militarized sonic presence over wartime Lebanon during 2006. Video excerpts of Clément Cogitore's operatic work *Les Indes Galantes* (2017) presented an energized, multi-racial KRUMP-style performance by Bintou Dembélé, Brahim Rachiki, and Igor Caruge that was, despite merely being a projection, truly mesmerizing. The Serbian artist Mila Turajlić explored archived

socialist solidarity newsreels made in the 1960s by journalist
Stefan Labudović in Tito's Yugoslavia. And a sobering and potent
work by artist Zuzanna Hertzberg explored the little-known and
frequently suppressed historical narrative of Polish Jewish women
in the uprisings against the Shoah in 1940s Eastern Europe.
Hertzberg's detailed archival banners were brought to life as she
diligently animated dozens of intersecting narratives involving
both individual and collective resistance at labor and death camps
in cities such as Warsaw, Kraków, Białystok, and Hrodna.[31]

Despite the inclusion of all this highly worthy work, the Berlin
Biennale primarily championed the self-critical introspective art that
could be argued to have been instrumental in opening up the very
possibility of a documenta 15 organized by artists situated at greater
distance of the global art scene. Indeed, one might even suggest
that the 2022 documenta and the Berlin Biennale each provided part
of a larger apparatus that allowed their visitors to glimpse
a counter-cultural zeitgeist of sorts, one that resists the hegemony
of mainstream capitalist, colonialist, and environmentally disastrous
politics, even if this newfangled assembly is not itself sufficient for
bringing about actual, fundamental social change. Still, the contrast
between the two exhibitions extends beyond what I have outlined
above, including simple quantitative terms whereby the sheer
multitude of documenta 15's participants raised a host of questions
and concerns about the nature of artistic production in relation to
the global market for contemporary art, an outcome of ruangrupa's
prioritizing of the so-called Global South.

By focusing on the art world's collective margins, documenta 15
generated a space for something quite alien to the contemporary
art marketplace: the unimpeded profusion of cultural production not
inhibited, or at least less pressured, by the rules of commerce. Take
the dizzying contribution made by Taring Padi, the multi-generational
Indonesian collective made up of communist and environmentalist-
oriented activist artists whose banner contained racially unsettling
images. Despite that work's disappearance, the group still presented
a cornucopia of visual protest activism that literally occupied an entire
Bauhaus-era building and its former indoor swimming pool at the
city's Hallenbad Ost location. The sheer vertiginous abundance
of Taring Padi's often burlesque painted, drawn, and printed figures—
social-realist flavored, sometimes affirmative, and other times angry

or deeply ironic—bolstered the anti-art market tenor of documenta 15. By overproducing works of art, a type of cultural object literally defined by its rarefied commodity status, Taring Padi and many other participants challenged the very notion of a uniquely collectable possession. To put it differently: when it comes to the parsimonious output of, say, a Jasper Johns, documenta 15 stands as an extreme opposite.

A similar, if not quite so prolific surfeit of stuff is evident with the group Britto Arts Trust whose installation resembled a countryside marketplace—brimming with a deluge of vegetables, fruits, bags of potatoes, and whole fish, all cast in ceramic by the Bangladesh-based collective. Inside the Karlsaue park, several boulder-sized bundles of compacted e-waste were parked near a two-story-high structure covered in used bales of fabric, here upcycled as building material. Inside, the Nest Collective's *Return to Sender* documentary explained—in a somewhat Berlin Biennale style—the negative impact of shipping such waste materials from the Global North to Africa, which impedes local economic development and results in environmental degradation. There were also mountains of compost with a working greenhouse (Más Arte Más Acción, Colombia), and a house-sized wall covered in hand-made Indonesian puppets (Yaya Coulibaly, Mali), as well as edible wheels of cheese related to Hito Steyerl's video piece that was—originally—part of the contribution by Fernando García Dory's INLAND collective and located inside the Natural History Museum.

There is another dimension to this overproduction that further impairs the normal conditions of contemporary fine art as a discrete and therefore specifically attributable and materially limited phenomenon. The excess yield displayed by many collectives that were part of documenta 15 extended well beyond visibly material surpluses into social networks distant from Kassel in both time and space. The collective agricultural project INLAND operates a radio station, art academy, study groups, and offers training programs for rural Spanish shepherds. It also publishes informational pamphlets about ecologically appropriate land use, and they make their own goat cheese. Más Arte Más Acción engages in environmental activism, hosts artistic residencies, research groups, and a school known as Chocó Base that investigates nature, music, regional knowledge and "creative laziness" among other topics in rural

Colombia. The Nest Collective hails from Nairobi, Kenya, and along with constructing art installations out of used consumables they organize Kitchen Conversations with Black and other immigrant groups in London, and a "Lift Festival" featuring theater and cinema, as well as dance spaces focused on non-binary people of "all origins, faiths and generations."[32] The Britto group "hub" is based in Dhaka and also offers residencies, as well as book-making workshops, video screenings, and has ventured into border politics by organizing meetings between Bangladeshi and Indian artists under the rubric of "No Man's Land." Meanwhile, Trampoline House has served as a meeting place in Denmark where refugees escaping human rights violations, war, and economic hardship can work with counselors, attend language classes, educational programs, and produce art exhibits. And finally, Taring Padi, who describe their mission as facilitating resistance against "elite discourse" by promoting a "populist or people's art," but also through directly organizing social and cultural organizations around a philosophy of anti-capitalism, mutual respect, and democratization, ideas that could only be spoken aloud after the fall of President Suharto's thirty-two-year-long military dictatorship fell in 1998.[33] And this is merely a fractional sampling of documenta 15's multitude of collective, expanded artistic practices.

Consider a third measure of the project's exorbitant amplitude: How does one plausibly quantify the precise number of actual participants who took part in documenta 15, including not only members of the initial fourteen invitees, but also their additional contributors? The task seems nearly impossible. Most of the fourteen each invited over fifty other additional participants, some of whom were collectives in their own right. The virtually unknowable list of documenta 15 contributors is not unlike what I call the dark matter of the art world—that invisible, unaccounted for mass of producers who literally ground and reproduce the entire system—was flowing giddily through the stalwart venues of the exhibitionary project in Kassel, like an ocean of suddenly charged and glistening particles.[34]

———

With this image of (temporarily) liberated artistic exuberance in mind, but also reminding ourselves of the dire, Walter White-like warnings made by various German media outlets, can we now take full measure of documenta 15's legacy? Probably not. However, some closing observations are possible and necessary.

Even as the exhibition remained in-process we heard a clearly exasperated ruangrupa admit that the "pressure on us to prove a negative—that we are not antisemitic—has been relentless."[35] In the weeks and months following the closing of documenta 15, ruangrupa has been condemned as reactionary by German born curator Dorothee Richter, while contrarily having been placed at the summit of the 2022 Art Power 100 list by the magazine *ArtReview*.[36] The documenta 15 debacle led to the far-Right-wing AfD party (Alternative for Germany) demanding a total defunding of the documenta exhibition platform, while the German Left has been split even more than before between those who support the type of decolonial discourse raised by ruangrupa, and those who believe that "any criticism of the Jewish state—or act of support for the Palestinian liberation struggle—is inherently and indisputably anti-Semitic."[37]

Meanwhile, the documenta organization itself has reacted by provisionally appointing Ferdinand von Saint André as its post-documenta 15 Managing Director, most notably because he specializes in legal matters related to German culture. Simultaneously, a December 2022 press release from the institution assured the art public—and no doubt the German state, gallerists, museums, collectors, policy makers and investors—that "in the spirit of a transparent process that builds on the knowledge gained from valuable experience" a special advisory committee has been formed to assist with the planning of documenta 16 in 2027. Who makes up this committee? Desperately, if not cynically, it consists of five past Artistic Directors reaching as far back as Rudi Fuchs of documenta 7 in 1982, while it is conspicuously absent of anyone from ruangrupa.[38]

There have indeed been consequences stemming from documenta 15, with many more ramifications to come as this critical platform moves forward, or just as, if not more likely, moves rearward.

1   In full disclosure, along with curator Olga Kopenkina I was invited to participate in an evening program as part of Tania Bruguera's installation INSTAR (Hannah Arendt Institute of Artivism). In addition, some parts of this essay first appeared in the September 22, 2022 edition of e-flux *Arts Agenda Reports* under the title "A short and incomplete history of 'bad' curating as collective resistance," see https://www.art-

agenda.com/criticism/491800/a-short-and-incomplete-history-of-bad-curating-as-collective-resistance (accessed March 1, 2023).

2   Lucy Lippard, "Trojan Horses: Activist Art and Power," in *Art after Modernism: Rethinking Representation*, edited by Brian Wallis (New York: New Museum of Contemporary Art, 1984), 341–58.

3   See the population statistics at https://www.citypopulation.de/en/germany/hessen/kassel_stadt/06611000__kassel/ (accessed March 1, 2023).

4   Anthony Gardner and Charles Green, "Post-North? Documenta11 and the Challenges of the 'Global Exhibition,'" *OnCurating*, issue 33, June 2017, available at https://www.on-curating.org/issue-33-reader/post-north-documenta11-and-the-challenges-of-the-global-exhibition.html#.YwJ_rOzMITt (accessed March 1, 2023).

5   Enwezor's team included, alongside himself, Carlos Basualdo, Ute Meta Bauer, Suzanne Ghez, Sarat Maharaj, Mark Nash, and Octavio Zaya.

6   See https://documenta-fifteen.de/en/ (accessed March 1, 2023).

7   Most notably documenta 14, led by Adam Szymczyck alongside close to forty others with some curatorial capacity or role, but also documenta 12, co-curated by Roger Buergel and Ruth Noack, and documenta 13, led by Carolyn Christov-Bakargiev together with a team of "agents" in a "core group" and beyond, as well as a range of "advisors."

8   "Documenta and anti-Semitism—Sloterdijk criticizes the art scene," *Time News*, June 25, 2022, available at https://time.news/documenta-and-anti-semitism-sloterdijk-criticizes-the-art-scene/ (accessed March 1, 2023).

9   Daniel Ben-Ami, "Identity politics is breathing new life into anti-Semitism," *Sp!ked,* July 3, 2022, available

at https://www.spiked-online.com/2022/07/03/identity-politics-is-breathing-new-life-into-anti-semitism/ (accessed March 1, 2023).

10   Josef Schuster, President of the Central Council of Jews in Germany, cited by Eric Langenbacher in "The Anti-Semitism Scandal at Documenta 15," website of the American Institute for Contemporary German Studies, Johns Hopkins University, July 20, 2020, available at https://www.aicgs.org/2022/07/the-anti-semitism-scandal-at-documenta-15/ (accessed March 1, 2023).

11   Samanth Subramanian, "A Radical Collective Takes Over One of the World's Biggest Art Shows," *New York Times Magazine*, June 9, 2022, updated June 17, 2022, available at https://www.nytimes.com/2022/06/09/magazine/ruangrupa-documenta.html?searchResultPosition=4 (accessed March 1, 2023).

12   As cited in "Top German art show starts amid anti-Semitism row," *Daily News*, June 21, 2022, available at https://www.hurriyetdailynews.com/top-german-art-show-starts-amid-anti-semitism-row-174716 (accessed March 1, 2023).

13   Kate Brown, "A Startling Exhibition on the History of Documenta Reveals the Political Moves—and Nazi Ties—of Its First Curators," *Artnet News* online, June 25, 2021, available at https://news.artnet.com/art-world/politics-art-documenta-1982336 (accessed March 1, 2023).

14   See Dorothee Richter, "Curatorial Commons? A Paradigm Shift," *OnCurating,* issue 54, November 2022, available at https://www.on-curating.org/issue-54-reader/curatorial-commons-a-paradigm-shift.html#.Y7ctrezMI-T (accessed March 1, 2023).

15   "Statement By Taring Padi On Dismantling 'People's Justice,'"

June 14, 2022, documenta 15 website, available at https://documenta-fifteen.de/en/news/statement-by-taring-padi-on-dismantling-peoples-justice/ (accessed March 1, 2023). See also a later reflection by the group in which they insist that they "should have known about this, and that was the mistake. It was utterly unnecessary and sloppy. We take responsibility for that and we go back to our principles about working together and learning together." Kate Brown interviewing members of Taring Padi in *Artnet News*, August 10, 2022, available at https://news.artnet.com/art-world/taring-padi-collective-interview-2155080 (accessed March 1, 2023).

16 Walter Benjamin, "Theses on the Philosophy of History," in *Critical Theory and Society: A Reader*, ed. Stephen Eric Bronner and Douglas MacKay Kellner (New York: Routledge, 2020), 255–63.

17 "The documenta is in ruins," Stefan Dege interviewing Dr. Mendel for *Quantara.de*, June 28, 2022, available at https://en.qantara.de/content/anti-semitism-at-documenta15-the-documenta-is-in-ruins (accessed March 1, 2023).

18 Daniele Muscionico, "Dismissal at the world art exhibition in Kassel," *Thurgauer Zeitung*, July 16, 2022, available at https://www.thurgauerzeitung.ch/kultur/documenta-entlassung-bei-der-weltkunstausstellung-in-kassel-antisemitismus-in-asien-ist-genauso-tabu-wie-antisemitismus-in-europa-ld.2318542 (accessed March 1, 2023).

19 Daniele Muscionico, "Goodbye Genius: Only Tribe Should Survive in Art," *Thurgauer Zeitung*, July 9, 2022, available at https://www.thurgauerzeitung.ch/kultur/documenta-goodbye-genie-in-der-kunst-sollen-nur-staemme-ueberleben-ld.2314760 (accessed March 1, 2023).

20 Alex Greenberger, "Jewish Art Space Shuts Down 'Rumors' It Was Disinvited from Documenta Amid Anti-Semitism Controversy," *ARTnews*, July 21, 2022, available at https://www.artnews.com/art-news/news/casa-do-povo-documenta-antisemitism-claims-1234634966/ (accessed March 1, 2023).

21 See Deutscher Bundestag document https://www.bundestag.de/dokumente/textarchiv/2019/kw20-de-bds-642892 (accessed March 1, 2023) And also here for full disclosure: I have supported cultural withdrawals as a way of pressuring Israel into granting full equality to Palestinian people in the occupied territories of Israel, just as I have actively confronted labor and human rights injustices in the UAE via my activism with Gulf Labor Coalition, which categorically refuses and resists all forms of racism and discrimination. See https://gulflabour.org/posts/ (accessed March 1, 2023).

22 Taylor Dafoe, "Vandals Attack a Kassel Arts Venue Where a Palestinian Group Is Set to Show During Documenta," May 31, 2022, *Artnet News*, available at https://news.artnet.com/art-world/Documenta-vanadalized-2124017 (accessed March 1, 2023).

23 Carlos Garrido Castellano, *Art Activism for an Anticolonial Future* (New York: State University of New York Press, 2021), 189.

24 Ibid., 192.

25 For more about the swarm politics of Occupy see my essay "OCCUPOLOGY, SWARMOLOGY, WHATEVEROLOGY…," *Art Journal Open*, January 5, 2012, available

at http://artjournal.collegeart.
org/?p=2395 (accessed March 1,
2023).

26 For more about the concept of the
phantom archive see my book, *The
Art of Activism and the Activism of Art*
(London: Lund Humphries, 2022).

27 First page of documenta 15 website,
https://documenta-fifteen.de/en/
(accessed March 1, 2023).

28 "What is Dayra," see https://dayra.net/
(accessed March 1, 2023).

29 See Katherine Gibson and the
Community Economics Research
Network website, available
at https://www.resilience.org/
stories/2021-04-01/katherine-gibson-
and-the-community-economies-
research-network/ (accessed March
1, 2023).

30 Mateusz Sapija, "Field Notes," *Art
& Education*, July 2022, available
at https://www.artandeducation.net/
schoolwatch/479069/field-notes-the-
question-of-funding-eltiqa-and-sada-
regroup-documenta-15 (accessed
March 1, 2023).

31 I witnessed the installation, but only
caught the performance later in New
York at the Center for Jewish History
as detailed in my blog post from
December 31, 2022, "Performing
the Archive: Zuzanna Hertzberg on
Individual and Collective Resistance
of Women During the Shoah," see
https://at.tumblr.com/gregsholette/
performing-the-archive-zuzanna-
hertzberg-on/rw7x2hztmmyu
(accessed March 1, 2023).

32 About The Nest Collective, see
https://www.thisisthenest.com/about
(accessed March 1, 2023).

33 Group websites listed in order:
INLAND at https://inland.org/about/
what-is-it/; Más Arte Más Acción at

https://www.masartemasaccion.
org/choco-como-escuela/; The Nest
at https://www.thisisthenest.com/;
Britto at http://brittoartstrust.org/;
Trampoline House at https://www.
trampolinehouse.dk/; Taring Padi
at https://www.taringpadi.com/ (all
accessed March 1, 2023).

34 Gregory Sholette, "Artists, Embrace
your Redundancy," Intro to "Dark
Matter," *Manifesta Journal*, #15,
2012, available at http://www.
gregorysholette.com/wp-content/
uploads/2022/07/Sholette-Manifesta-
15-Journal-Artists-Embrace-
Your-Redundancy-in-Manifesta-
Journal-15-2012.pdf (accessed
March 1, 2023).

35 Speech by Ade Darmawan of
ruangrupa from July 6, 2022,
available at https://documenta-
fifteen.de/en/news/speech-by-
ade-darmawan-ruangrupa-in-the-
committee-on-culture-and-media-
german-bundestag-july-6-2022/
(accessed March 1, 2023).

36 Richter, "Curatorial Commons?
A Paradigm Shift."

37 Hebh Jamal questions this position
by pointing out that, "Germany has
succeeded in making any and all
support for Palestinian liberation, and
speech against Israeli occupation,
if not criminal, at least taboo," in
her op-ed, "Germany is targeting
post-colonial thinkers for a reason,"
Aljazeera, December 12, 2022,
available at https://www.aljazeera.
com/opinions/2022/12/12/germany-is-
threatened-by-postcolonialism-for-a-
reason (accessed March 1, 2023).

38 From documenta press release dated
November 11, 2022, available at
https://www.documenta.de/en/press
(accessed March 1, 2023).

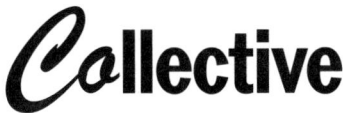ollective

Use in a Sentence
"We are a collective."
"We work collectively."
"We have a collective practice."

Synonyms
Assembly
Shared
Group

TAB definition
A collective is a group of people—maybe an organization or
a company. A group of people with a collective purpose or mindset,
working toward the same thing, who chose to make use of their
differences together.

"Collective" describes a sense of not being alone. It may refer to the collective experiences of a group, or a shared thought, experience, or feeling.

Collectives have group dynamics. They share strengths to fulfill their needs from and with each other.

What's the difference between a collective and a cult?

The word "collective" describes a type of collaboration in which you try to let everyone work in ways that are individually right for them, not ways that are imposed by someone. It suggests a non-hierarchical structure.

A collective space sounds like a more democratic space in which people work together without a dominating power structure. Power and agency are distributed. It's a space where no one holds ownership, everyone is equal, and everyone has access.

In our workshops in Helsinki, the discussion about how we can create open and inclusive spaces was key. Used as an adverb, "collective" action implies political mass action—striking, protesting, the powerful acts of a group taking power and using the power of many people being together.

In the Teen Advisory Board we are working toward a collective goal. We came with our own predispositions and aims, but now we work together toward the same thing, even if we are not necessarily all working in the same way, or toward something that affects everyone in the same way.

A collective needs to decide to come together. That may happen by coincidence, but you have to be able to come together to decide to be together. A group becomes a collective when its members make a conscious decision and choose to see each other as equals. A group can assemble, but they aren't a collective until they choose to be.

It's easy to be on the outside and label a group a collective when that group isn't necessarily thinking that way. You may be in a group that acts collectively without realizing you are. But sometimes people group other people together, and think of the group as a "collective," which can go hand in hand with political stereotypes. The difference between someone labeling a group and a group of people labeling themselves a collective depends on whether they have a straightforward shared goal or intention.

Use it as a Verb / How to DO It .

As a verb, you can talk about practicing collectively. A collective practice that we have at PTAB involves "check-ins" and "check-outs": making sure to collect input, ideas, and views from everyone in an equal and fair way. Collective practice involves establishing some sort of mission statement, which sets out what people will contribute and how. A collective practice can be a condition or a norm that you share.

ESTABLISHED DEFINITIONS

Tate glossary: "Loosely defined, an art collective is a group of artists working together to achieve a common objective."

Oxford Learner's Dictionary: "a singular noun, such as committee or team, that refers to a group of people, animals or things and, in British English, can be used with either a singular or a plural verb. In American English it must be used with a singular verb."

Cambridge Dictionary: "Adjective: done or shared by every member of a group: a collective action/effort/decision. 'It will require a collective effort from government, providers, and the media to meet our goals.' Collective responsibility/rights. 'All directors take collective responsibility for board decisions.'"

RELATED WORDS

Collaboration.

Understanding.
When we visited a lady at the island in Helsinki, we were shown her textile art. At first it was difficult to see or understand this type of art, but after having her explain and educate us on her culture and the reason behind it, it was easier to reflect and see the beauty of it.

Solidarity.

Collective effort.

Cooperation.

Connection.
When we tried out different activities together, it felt like we connected as a group. It didn't feel like anyone cared about how unusual the activity was. It was a way for the workshop presenter to make us explore different forms of breathing and sound making. It didn't only make a connection between the TAB members, but also between the TAB groups and the presenter.

Independent.

This text is an extract from the section "TAB 2022 Glossary" in How do we know? Institutional listening and young agency in the arts *(2022). The glossary was created through a process of collective and individual writing during the workshop "If Culture Was A House, Then Language Was The Key," conducted by Ina Hagen and Sol Archer with members of the Teen Advisory Boards of PRAKSIS and Index, Oslo and Stockholm. The co-authors are Aisha Berge, Alcina Nancy Munene Persson, Anahita Mishra, Ari Sigurdarson, Dugagjin Osmanaj, Emil Temim, Fariha Fatima Malik, Felix Sjögren, Gard Møller-Johansen, Ilwaad H. Mahamed, Luna Sackett, Malin Issa, Mey-Thip Mortensen, Sarikazaman Ullah, Sujani Sutharsan, and Vigo Roth.*

Not Going It Alone:

*A C*onversation

Gerrie van Noord / Paul O'Neill

Gerrie van Noord: Looking at developments over time, there is quite a discourse on artistic collectives and group practices but much less around curatorial practices in which collaboration and/or collective working is a central characteristic. One of the issues is maybe how to acknowledge who collaborates with whom, for what reasons, and how we name or label things. Before discussing these aspects, maybe we could simply start with how this book came about.

> **Paul O'Neill:** apexart approached me for a text for a publication on collaborative curating, for which I reworked an existing essay, first published in *Art Monthly* in the early 2000s, and extended about a decade later. apexart has increasingly worked with curatorial collectives, groups of artists and curators, or groups of curators working

together to formulate an exhibition proposal. The impetus
was an increase in applicants to their Open Calls with
a clear tendency toward group work or collective work. Having
received a range of contributions, apexart were very keen
that this book would not just valorize personal narratives
or self-branding approaches, so they asked me to take on
the project as editor, where my text would frame ideas
in a wider context. Elizabeth Larison's introduction expands
on the specifics from apexart's perspective.

I see collective or group work as most clearly defined
in artistic practices, and as all artistic work is somehow
curatorial, but perhaps less overt in some practices. Art
and curating as collaborative work started to become
increasingly prominent in the early 2000s, when multiple
histories of curatorial and artistic practices emerged,
and the relationship between group work and this murky
territory around who does what and how, and why certain
artists become visible—often under influence of market
mechanisms—and others don't, became a focus point.

When I wrote that initial text in the early 2000s, and
re-rewrote it for this book, one thing I firmly maintain is that
we never work alone. One of my key concerns is how
you articulate that not working alone and demystify the way
in which we work with others while not mythologizing or
romanticizing group, collective, or collaborative work as the
natural outcome of a process of critique of individualism
or individual authorship. In the shift toward the collaborative
or collective turn in the late 1990s and early 2000s, certain
collectives were highlighted while others were not and that
also raised questions for me.

GvN: There are comprehensive summaries of the nuanced differences
between various kinds of artistic collaboration and collectivity,
and where and how they might and might not overlap. You reworked
that early 2000s text for a thematic issue of *Manifesta Journal*,
around 2010, in which a range of voices explored what curatorial
collaboration might entail and what it could lead to. However,

in that embrace of plurality, stepping away from the singular and individual in practice, there seems to have been a replacement of one for the other without the language to describe what unfolds changing all that much. This makes me wonder whether "collaboration" and "collective" are themselves generic umbrella terms that mask the complexities that lie behind them.

Which is why, when looking at your text for this publication, I suggested we revisit your initial submission and consider whether in the expanding debate around group and collective and collaborative work, the terms have shifted at all. Several contributions to this volume speak to that real tension between changes in practice and how they are then talked about, which is reflected in public perception and critical reception; think for instance of documenta 15, which Gregory Sholette expands on in his essay here. Is the complexity of practices mirrored in their critiques, or are we all still struggling to articulate pluralistic diversity and complexity in what we see or encounter?

PON: Critique of single authorship, and replacing the singular with the plural, or the singular with versions of the plural, also emerged in the 1990s in relation to relational practices, and the various biennials taking on the collective global curating as a space of the creative multitude, cultural pluralism and multiple identity formations. The early 2000s were also a pivotal period because of the incorporation of the collaborative as a methodology within institution-building, as critique of older models and as part of newly emergent forms. Trying to distinguish between what constitutes a collective and what constitutes collaboration, collaboration for me is much more a methodology of how you work with others and how you then make that process of working with others apparent in how you inscribe the practice. I understand a collective as a group of people coming together with a common agenda or urgent goal in mind; often there is an investment in instituting change, or transformation, or a common ideology. This is why collectives are often more a mechanism of defense, or a force for change that uses collaboration as a methodology. Some collectives work very collaboratively, some do not work collaboratively at all.

In trying to more comprehensively disclose or understand the rationale for the shift toward collective work or a collaboration, it's also useful to realize it's been happening for forever. It's not new. What has changed is that a different language, a different vocabulary has emerged, or is constantly emerging, indoctrinating, and inscribing, and in a way valorizing, certain ways of working collectively above others. That is the moment we're in now, but it's still subsumed within a culture of individualism and superseded by a focus and emphasis on the self and self-care and being together alone. This language didn't come from nowhere, it comes from an emphasis on the self, and the neoliberalization of the self via social media image projection. To project oneself as being collective, individually, is an incredible promotional tool for many media savvy people, including artists and curators. I'm talking across disciplines, from the visual to pop music, they all have facilitated a kind of a self-image that's ultimately a portrayal of some sort of idea of the collective or of something bigger than the self that is really situated in individualism. This drive toward the collective as a space of rethinking our space of critique is still very submerged within a bigger field of selfishness.

There is also a distinction with certain curators taking over institutions in the early 2000s—like Maria Lind at Kunstverein Munich, or Charles Esche at the Rooseum in Malmö, or Catherine David at Witte de With in Rotterdam, Hans Ulrich Obrist at Musée d'art Moderne de la Ville de Paris, or Hou Hanru at the San Francisco Art Institute, or the significance of Thelma Golden in 2000 starting as Deputy Director at The Studio Museum in Harlem—in a bid to debate the expanding role of the art institution beyond exhibition-making, accounting for an expanded practice, including attention for identity politics and the importance

of archiving such practice. There is also the significance of
curatorial initiatives such as INIVA, established already in
1994, or Asia Art Archive, founded in 2000, around the same
time as globally nomadic curators initiating curatorial project
like the Palais de Tokyo in Paris.

Alongside these curators, you saw artists claiming
a certain investment in collaboration or in group work
entering institutions to try and transform them into critical
structures and make the collaborative methodology
apparent within those institutions, or across a range of
emergent new biennials in the first decade of this century.
Most cases were short-lived experiences that were part
of "new institutionalism," as it was called then, which
became a diluted form of collaborative work. By the late
1990s and early 2000s there was an increasing number
of new cooperative-oriented institutions as diverse and
geographically dispersed as Parasite in Hong Kong, or the
nomadic If I Can't Dance… in Amsterdam, Chimurenga
in Cape Town, Bétonsalon in Paris, What, How and for
Whom in Zagreb, Raw Material in Dakar, or Casco and
BAK in Utrecht, or Grupo Ectétera in Argentina. They and
many others led the way to shifting curatorial work away
from authorial structures toward modes of group work.

One of the problems with this replacement of the singular
with the plural is how the plural came to be seen as good
and the singular as bad. For me a greater engagement
with what is good or bad practice within pluralities, and
this distinction between the collective as a kind of form of
instituting and collaboration as methodology, or different
methodologies or different ways of working together,
ethically or unethically, is important. Discussions around
these distinctions started in the early 2000s, with resistance
to the idea of collaboration or collective work as necessarily
a good thing emerging. There were also people like
SUPERFLEX and others articulating collective work as
a conduit to the art market because it was perceived as
something that was more diffuse and more redistributable,

as an alternative to the focus on the individual or working with a singular artist.

I think it's also important to acknowledge how necessary it has been within my own writing practice to collaborate with people, including yourself, and to make that more apparent within editorial structures and within collaborative structures. How do you create spaces within your own work to enable your collaborators to do their thing, and support your own thing? That has been quite important for me. The three books that I worked on while at Bard—*The Curatorial Conundrum*, *How Institutions Think* and *Curating After the Global*—were in a way trying to find out how by involving multiple editors and multiple authors you can almost disappear as an editor, as author, within that matrix of other people's positions. These anthologies are spaces of constant negotiation, renegotiation, and reenactment of recognition, with a breakdown of clarity of whose words and whose voice they are. That is what's great about anthologies—when you're working very closely with the authors, putting in that effort.

GvN: What you're hinting at is indeed a dichotomy between practice and its articulation, how we talk about it, and it's therefore useful to think about the different positions within this book, with contributors situated in different parts of the world engaged in different kinds of problematics. From their geographically, politically, socially specific positions, they present their views, but they do so in response to a specific invitation, from you as an editor, for a specific context, this book, in a process of writing, with me as another editor. Collaboratively we try to figure out what can be said and how, and that contributes to a thinking about ways of collaborating that is specific but also becomes part of this wider thinking through publishing.

That's why I see the writing for and publication in books like these as a very collaborative process too, where value lies in working carefully, going back and forth and back and forth again. In the case of this book, Elizabeth also entering the equation, with a different perspective, coming from a different position, questioning how certain

things were said and why, and how that might land with readers
in other contexts. That process of articulation through reflection,
response, a further response, a further reiteration is a slow process.
The embrace of that process as iterative, as productive, for me
is an integral part of articulation. In the case of your text, that meant
taking into account the starting point as well as the first revisit
and then add another revisit for this anthology; when most other
texts had come in, thinking whether it made sense to work on it
again, where it was not about trying to cover all bases, but rather
about stepping into that collaborative space of figuring out what was
important to say and how now, compared to the early 2000s or
a decade ago. There was a clarity of thinking in your initial ideas on
collective ways of working, particularly in artistic practices, while
collaborative and group working are here considered through
a more curatorial lens. Now we're in the early 2020s, other ideas
have entered the field—not only about collaborative and collective
working, but also notions like "the curatorial," underlining the
complexity of collaboration as something that isn't just one thing,
that does something very specific, trying to open that up…

PON: That's very much what comes across in the cluster
or constellation of positions, or collaborative imaginaries in
the essays we received. Each text has an internal logic or
an internal conversation about the curatorial as collective or
collaborative work but is here situated it in a wider, global
context. Within my own essay, I discuss paradigmatic
collectives, like General Idea, Group Material, and Art &
Language. These collectives or artists' groups were being
reconsidered two decades ago as important to a rethinking
of the "genius" of the artist and individualism. Group
Material and General Idea both emerged at a very political
moment, with the AIDS crisis and queer political activist
agendas in the 1980s. They need to be seen in relation to
the specifics of that decade, not only in terms of the
concerns, issues, and questions they were asking, but also
what they were doing in the ways of working together
and ways of thinking about distributed practice. There
were also numerous other hybrid art collectives globally
active during the early to mid 1980s such as Godzilla:

Asian American Arts Network, or Gutai Group in Japan, IRWIN from former Yugoslavia, or the UK-based Black Audio Film Collective, who were testing collaborative modes of co-production, while operating within the global networks of art and exhibition production within and beyond non-Western global perspectives.

The exhibition *Collective Creativity* by WHW at the Fridericianum in Kassel (2005) was an important marker of this increased interest. More recent events, such as WHW being appointed directors of the Kunsthalle Vienna (in 2019), and ruangrupa being appointed as the first curatorial collective to take over documenta in 2022, underline a different shift toward collective work within bigger institutions. In addition, appointing a non-Western curatorial collective for documenta and them inviting other curatorial and artistic collectives as part of their methodology, their presentation of a new global order…, these are important moments to reflect on. But while the *Collective Creativity* show was very much applauded, and announced this emergent agenda, WHW becoming directors in Vienna was very problematic for the institution and for that collective, for lots of different reasons. Similarly, the kickback toward documenta 15, with various political agendas coming together, demonstrated that changes aren't a smooth or clear processes. The texts in this book try and trace the complex convergences of this moment as something quite different to what was happening at the beginning of this century, while making connections with other important practices and conversations happening more on the fringes of these more dominant art-worldly narratives.

GvN: Thinking about that difference, galvanizing a group of people around a common cause that underpinned working as a collective in the 1980s as you outline in your text, clearly runs into trouble in the context of the quite regressive political, social tendencies that we find ourselves among, globally. For a long time, there was a sense that collaborative and collective ways of working provided an alternative and there were spaces that could be occupied beyond or alongside the market. Over the last 25 years there has been a diversification, both in artistic and curatorial practices, where those ways of working could manifest themselves. The accumulation or possibility of what some people still perceive as alternative ways of operating, and the problems surrounding them entering the more institutionalized, mainstream arenas like documenta has highlighted that there is still great apprehension, exacerbated by our current challenging times.

Picking up on a previous point; the perceived value of what people do is also tied to those articulations, and what you called inscriptions, like yours around Group Material and General Idea, but going back and asking again: what happened there? Revisiting is a wider phenomenon in the art world now; you see it in the amount of people reflecting on the 1990s. Wondering: what was the value? How can we look at it from today's perspective? Which is part of an ongoing process of articulation and re-articulation. I see an incredible value in continuing to do that, particularly because of those regressive responses to WHW and documenta 15. What was the outcome of that way of working then? What could it be now? What has shifted, what has broadened out, or hasn't? There is a clear impetus to keep trying, both in practice and in reflection, but maybe slightly differently.

> **PON:** I think the shift was not from one system of artistic production to another, but more one of different ways of imagining how we could work together, and how to really embed such methodological processes within institutional reimagining. The art world excludes, or at least makes it less apparent, that documenta, and many other curatorial projects, are a collective endeavor too. Every documenta that's seemingly directed by one visible director has always been realized via different forms of group work. The valorizing machine tries to erase considerable chunks of such histories—where ruangrupa's collective of collectives, and their unique geopolitical contexts and activist agendas, including different feminist, queer, ecological, environmental, human rights agendas, and so on, are met with resistance. This intersectionality was very palpable, where it wasn't

one political agenda superseding another, allowing for
a certain kind of messiness. Think also of the Turner Prize
deciding to award its prize to so-called collectives; it must
be very difficult for the institution to understand how their
decisions are being made because they're not given
the time or the space to even be able to imagine what they
could do collectively and collaboratively.

GvN: Early critiques of collaborative working and socially engaged
art railed against the attention for process over product. Within
institutions, and entities like documenta, the lack of time always
leads to a tension because at some stage the doors need to open,
something needs to be made visible. The Turner Prize is interesting
in that sense: it's a celebration, but a celebration of what, and for
whom?—to stick to the Ws. The question embedded in the name
WHW indicates a kind of grappling with bigger concerns around
what is being produced—for whom indeed? In that sense, groups
like WHW and Raqs have taken on the challenge and seem to be
able to endure in different kinds of contexts and really stay with the
problematics that their ways of working highlight. They've stuck with
it as a mode of practice and with being articulate about not doing
this within just their collective but stepping into situations that broaden
the potential of collective and collaborative thinking. I am using these
words interchangeably on purpose here, because sometimes it is
more collaborative, and sometimes it is explicitly collective. That's
an ongoing process of taking time and committing to the time that is
needed, which is of course a luxury that isn't always available.

PON: In relation to the durational or temporal process,
what's clear for me is this saturation of time in the exhibition
as form. The exhibition is the materialization of a process
of gathering, or of being in contradiction to one another;
the exhibition is a space where these contradictions and
disagreements, or antagonism or agonisms are on display
or exposed in some way and then debated and discussed.
That means using the exhibition as a kind of discursive
space, or as a discursive site, within which the process
guides or takes shape regardless of its form, a moment when
these things are discussed and debated. That is also

something that emanates from collaborative work, which you see with General Idea and Group Material: when you look at those genealogies, you see an investment in the exhibition as a space of saturation, as a space of concentration, where cooperative, collective, and group thinking and working come together, are formulated, or articulated, or (re)presented. This interest or investment in the exhibition as a space within which time gathers its form or concentrates is relatively novel and relatively emergent still. That is where this idea of "the curatorial" becomes a space of inquiry for both artists and curators.

In the last three years, the notion of care and togetherness have of course become prevalent, whereas togetherness and care have been completely lacking—not only within our own lives, but also within systems of governance and their institutions, such as healthcare, mental healthcare, travel, mobility, water, and other resources. All of which are part of being together. The over-emphasis on care in the art world creates this romantic idea of the art world as a space within which care can happen, while it's not happening anywhere else. This is why Bonaventure Soh Bejeng Ndikung's text within this book is very important in terms of arguing for a nuanced critique or care as a generic curatorial term, where an etymology of curating as care for art, artists, or the world is quite delusionary given the market-driven forces of curators' careers in an art world rife with competition, injustice, inequality, and an imbalanced relationship with the real needs of others. That is something that requires differentiation, further investigation, extensive debate, and a reimagining of the specific types of workspaces encapsulated in and supported by or through collective labor, or spaces of exhibition, or cooperative making processes.

I think it was also important to mark this post-documenta 15 moment in relation to other cooperative, collaborative, and collective projects happening elsewhere in the world that do not have the same visibility or the same representability within contemporary discourses—as those evoked in poetic reflections by María Berríos, Pip Day, and Sofía Olascoaga; or embedded collective projects in Mexico, such as Nina Möntmann describes; or in former Eastern Europe, as Agnieszka Pindera outlines in her survey of a longer historical trajectory of curatorial collaborations in that part of the world; or the work of the tranzit curatorial network (represented here in the text by Nikolett Erőss and Eszter Lázár), who have also been thinking about collective and group work in contexts other than that of the West; or the crystallization of the potential of collaborative work in Ghana and West Africa, as highlighted by Serubiri Moses; and the reflections from younger generations, such as the Index and PRAKSIS Teen Advisory Boards. This book is a way of exhibiting these different temporalities, and these different geopolitical perspectives. We should approach this collection with a lot of caution too, because what these texts describe is not all part of the same context, they're not all speaking to the same moment, or not even to the same understanding of collective curatorial work and collaborative practices.

GvN: Most of the texts are not fully resolved in terms of the potential of the ideas and projects discussed. What they all do do, in their descriptions and critical analysis of collaborative and collective work— in Ghana and West Africa, Latin America, former Eastern Europe, as well as more established Western perspective—is offer a range of critical propositions. They offer ways of thinking and doing "otherwise," another now often-used umbrella term that needs specificity. Individually, and collectively they look at the frameworks in which these critical propositions unfold and also outline the limitations of what particular situations—socially, politically, geographically—offer that can possibly be unraveled, unpicked, and re-articulated elsewhere.

1   Paul O'Neill, Simon Sheikh, Lucy Steeds, Mick Wilson, eds., *Curating After the Global: Roadmaps for the Present* (Cambridge, MA: MIT Press, with CCS Bard and Luma Foundation, 2019); Paul O'Neill, Simon Sheikh, Lucy Steeds, and Mick Wilson, eds., *How Institutions Think: Between Contemporary Art and Curatorial Discourse* (Cambridge, MA: MIT Press, 2017); and Paul O'Neill, Lucy Steeds, and Mick Wilson, eds. *The Curatiorial Conundrum: What to Study? What to Research? What to Practice?* (Cambridge, MA: MIT Press, with CCS Bard and Luma Foundation, 2016).

*B*eyond *H*ierarchy:

Articulating Collaboration

Gerrie van Noord

*Rather than concretizing and containing a single
person's authorship [collaboration] disperses
it into the history of the networks of communications
that went into its making.*
— Raqs Media Collective[1]

In an early reflection on the increase of collaborative artistic
practices, Maria Lind argues for a distinction between what she calls
"single" and "double" collaboration. In the former "the author remains
alone and contributions of others are towards the realisation of
an idea," whereas in the latter "collaboration takes place both on the
level of the author, with the formulation of the idea, and also in the
realisation of the work."[2] The issue with this distinction between idea
and execution is not only one of hierarchy, of attributing greater value
to one over the other. It also positions ideas as more or less fully
formed once enunciated. In my experience though, ideas tend to shift
and expand in dialogue with others, as well as in their doing, making,
and realizing. If we follow this train of thought, any materialization
of an idea is but one among a spectrum of possibilities in a fluid
process. However, what happens when people come together, are
together and work together, to paraphrase Lind, is in the discourse

often overshadowed by a continued focus on *who* comes together *with whom*. In this brief but quote-heavy text, in which I refer to others' thinking to try and articulate my own, I want to consider the terms we use in the discourse around collaborative, collective, group work, and their implications.

Critical debate tends to situate such work as generic alternatives or forms of resistance to systemic issues, some of which are specific to the art world while others are experienced far beyond.[3] Groupings of group work on the one hand demonstrate an increased understanding that something is to be gained from joining forces, resulting in a ubiquity of "not going it alone" as the production of this book itself highlights. On the other hand, many summative overviews of worthy exemplars end up smoothing over the broad range of models, rationales, and specific contexts in which working with others unfolds, and more importantly, how. Despite decades of group, collective, and collaborative work behind us, this "flattening out" of this diversity underlines the importance of trying to articulate this how.

Around the same time as Lind and Raqs articulated their observations, agenda-setting definitions of "the curatorial" emerged, in which collaboration is an integral characteristic. Lind situates "the curatorial" as a "qualitative concept," operating as "an active catalyst, generating twists, turns, and tensions,"[4] and Irit Rogoff emphasizes its potential as a "knowledge event" that evolves in the convergence of different existing knowledges.[5] Many others have expanded and added nuance to the scope of what it may comprise since.[6] However, when thinking, speaking, or writing about the plurality of group work, "who" is really accounted for, "who" is actually being referred to in the "we" of any collaboration in art, curatorial practice, and their attendant discourses?

As Sarah Ahmed keenly observed in the 1990s, "who" is speaking is "a marker of a specific location from which the subject writes."[7] What is more, for Ahmed, "refusal to enter the discourse as an empirical subject [...] may finally translate into a universalising mode of discourse" that in turn "negates the specificity of its own inscription."[8] It is arguably precisely this tension between the generic and the specific that haunts so much curatorial literature. Not long after Ahmed's astute comment, John Roberts wonders whether "collaboration [is] essentially a post-autonomous condition" or instead "the space where autonomy (or rather the necessary fiction of autonomy) is defended and implemented."[9] This fiction of autonomy hints more widely at the persistent contradictions between "the doing" in artistic and curatorial practices and how they are described, inscribed, and ultimately historicized.

Contemplating similar concerns, in a 2013 interview Marion von Osten asks: "why don't other people name all their collaborators?"[10] Indeed, why don't they? Framing her question about this lack, Von Osten refers to conventions in film, in which everyone—from producer to runner, from lead actor to costume designer—is credited at the end. While this may at first glance seem a more generous and inclusive way of acknowledging the diversity of roles and positions that together realize highly complex work, one could equally argue that naming everyone in a certain order while specifying their individual contribution, as film credits do, perpetuates the foregrounding of certain positions over others, and thereby underlines their assumed greater value. Highlighting similar concerns, Rogoff has gone as far as suggesting that when we speak and write about art and curating with terms like "'art," "audience," "curator," and "institution," our vocabulary is largely "evacuated of meaning."[11] Raqs Media Collective in turn have argued that the "figure of the individuated artist and the solitary intellectual is […] a momentary blip in the long human history of dividuated [sic] practices and dialogic forms of thought."[12]

As artists' and curators' practices are always heavily networked and collaborative—often with other kinds of practitioners[13]—why do descriptions of collaboration, group, or collective work still acknowledge, and by extension attribute (greater) value to only a few individualized positions? Given the shared questions around how collaboration is discussed, it is worth considering what the ramifications are of the continued use of a limited set of individualized labels, especially when their connotations no longer match how so many practices operate. Does the use of such terms effectively uphold the systemic hierarchies belying the fundamental nature of the interactions and connections many are trying to articulate? Rather than listing everyone in every constellation and expanding on the range of individual and positions involved, might finding different ways of describing collaboration be a more productive way of moving beyond this conundrum?

It would be disingenuous to pretend though that attempts at nuancing descriptions of collaborative modes of working have not been undertaken. Rather than proposing ways that might help us step away of from the focus on who collaborates with whom, such discussions have often preoccupied themselves with the form such work takes. The distinction between curatorial and so-called "paracuratorial" work, for instance, in which the exhibition as modality is set in contrast with other modalities, introduces another hierarchy—of what should be perceived as "proper" curatorial work and what shouldn't.[14] Observing the backlash against such thinking, Tara McDowell suggests that "[t]he distinction between discursive curating and a regressive 'artwork-first model of curation' rests on shaky ground."[15] Her comment is a response to Paul O'Neill's observation of the emergence of a "conservative urge to return to the more stable distinctions between the work of the artist, the curator, the educator, the public" that followed the apparent abandonment of the exhibition as medium.[16] Trying to break through both the hierarchy among individualized positions and the modalities of work they engage in, he posits that "the curatorial" is "a field of praxis that resists categorical resolution, conceived instead as a constellation of activities that do not wish to fully reveal themselves."[17] While the term "constellation" is situated here as "an ever-shifting and dynamic cluster of changing elements that are always resisting reduction to a single common denominator," it still leaves us somewhat in the descriptive dark as to what happens among the range of praxes that come together.[18]

To explore a potential alternative, I want to consider Isabelle Stengers's notion of "ecology of practices."[19] The malleability of Stengers's ideas offers a way of thinking *around* individual contributions and contributors, while never undermining their distinctive relevance and agency per se, instead homing in on what happens in their convergences. Stengers argues that "[p]ractices are interdependent, each needs others in order to exist and expand," which sounds deceptively simple and straightforward.[20] However, as outlined above, this interdependence is not always reflected in what we read about collaboration in art and curating. Despite shifting ways of working and critical reflections emphasizing they do, a specific descriptive temporal linear order—starting with the artist, followed by the curator, and then the audience, with

"participants" sometimes added in the mix—prevails. I suggest
that Stengers's notion of "ecology of practices" enables a rethink
on both the systemic (ecology) and the individual level (practitioners)
at the same time. In addition, it may help us bypass the pitfalls
of the binary "them and us," and free us from having to ensure
everyone is acknowledged while being kept in their hierarchical
place nonetheless.[21]

For Stengers, an "ecology of practices" "accentuate[s] positive
divergence," which she describes as "oppos[ing] any ordering,
any derivation of the 'each' from its place in the ensemble, just as
contemporary ecology opposes the idea of an order of nature," which
is not too dissimilar to some of the key tenets of "the curatorial"
as outlined earlier.[22] Lind's initial definition of "the curatorial" hinges
of the idea of "agonism"—a term introduced by Chantal Mouffe,
which considers disagreement, often around social-political
concerns, as a productive force for change. My proposition is that
Stengers's "positive divergence" as a default condition of an "ecology
of practices" offers a broader alternative for thinking through the
potential of collaborative, collective, and group work, enabling us
to shift the primary focus toward what happens or unfolds between
Lind's coming together, being together, and working together, and
Rogoff's emergence of the "event of knowledge." As such, it could
help us articulate what is often a missing, or certainly flattened link
in reflexive accounts of such work. My suggestion is therefore not
in opposition to either Lind's or Rogoff's or others' ideas, rather an
"ecology of practices" offers and expansion that allows for greater
complexity and depth.

When Lind expands on "the curatorial" as a series of
"signification processes and relationships between objects, people,
places, ideas,"[23] she focuses on the art world and skirts past how
these processes often bring in practitioners rooted elsewhere, and
who have their own histories, traditions, and conventions that do
"work" on others in moments of encounter. In spite of "accept[ing]
the need for different practitioners to weave relations around
issues of common interest," Stengers rightly highlights how distinct
discourses tend to "dismember these issues with their diverging
demands."[24] This goes some way in explaining why, in descriptions
of collaborative projects with different kinds of practitioners—
including artists and curators—they tend to remain perceived as

distinct, as not connected beyond temporary mobilization around common interests. In addition to the generally upheld distinction between "them and us," there is often a clear sense of those on the "inside" and those on the "outside"—with "participants," "communities," and "publics" situated on or just outside the porous boundary between the art world and the rest of the world.[25]

If we were to apply Stengers's ideas to collaborative and collective work, we would no longer have to focus on just identifying individual achievements. Instead, specific positions and their individual agency could be situated as always dependent on and co-determined through interactions *with* others. This is not to say that individual agency as traditionally understood—driven by desires, needs, hopes, intentions, and expectations, but also considerations of conventions and traditions, among many other (f)actors—does not exist. However, thinking through Stengers's lens of an "ecology of practices"—in which the infinite ecology of multiple practices or fields already comprises the slightly less expansive whole of each individual practice—could be argued to exceed or surpass individual agency in the momentary "passing on" between practitioners.

Whereas Ahmed draws our attention to the relevance of who speaks, Stengers underlines the interconnection between a practice and the landscape in which it is being practiced—and by extension the interconnection of all actors and agents within and beyond—the complexity of which acts on who is speaking. Considering each practice as part of a complex ecology, and often multiple ecologies at the same time, would also help us acknowledge practices are never just one thing—irrespective of whether they are considered collective, group, or collaborative—but are always a conglomerate of interconnected roles and tasks between which we all oscillate all the time already.[26]

Where does the foregrounding of being part of an "ecology of practices" leave us in terms of the distinction between ideas and execution and single and double collaboration and claims of authorship that Lind outlined? And where would it leave us in how we articulate our descriptions and critical reflections? Building on Stengers's idea of "positive divergence," we could continue to recognize who collaborates with whom but also situate ideas and execution as malleable and interconnected parts of ongoing processes between those credited. If we were to embrace any practice as part of ongoing sequences of "passing on" within a field and with practitioners from other fields, the question of "who" is speaking may take on another weight, requiring less emphasis on the singular who, and suggest we consider them as but one who in an ecology of whos, plural. The interplay between ideas and execution, and the process of exchange impacting on both, might come into view as an extended game of musical chairs, without the need for identifying precisely who was the originator in a specific temporal order. Thinking about the interconnected processes of inviting, articulating, editing, rewriting, re-editing, and publishing of this book, this may lead to seemingly less traditional narratives with clearly identifiable singular protagonists, where group, collective and collaboration are positioned as always plural and malleable.

1   Raqs Media Collective, "Additions, Subtractions: On Collectives and Collectivities," *Manifesta Journal*, #8, 2009–10, 8. Raqs operate intermittently as an artists' and a curatorial collective.

2   Maria Lind, "The Collaborative Turn," in *Taking the Matter into Common Hands: On Contemporary Art and Collaborative Practices*, ed. Johanna Billing, Maria Lind, and Lars Nilsson (London: Black Dog Publishing, 2007), 27. A significant expansion of this text was published as "Complications; On Collaboration, Agency and Contemporary Art," in *Public, Art, Culture, Ideas*, no. 39, spring 2009, 53–73.

3   In his essay "Beyond Trending: Group Practices in Art and Curating" in this volume, Paul O'Neill covers various genealogies of practice and discourse over time, which is why I refrain from further references here.

4   Maria Lind, "The Curatorial," *Artforum*, October 2009, 103.

5   Irit Rogoff in conversation with Beatrice von Bismarck, "Curating/ Curatorial," in *Cultures of the Curatorial*, ed. Beatrice von Bismark,

Jörn Schafaff, and Thomas Weski (Berlin: Sternberg, 2012), 22–23.

6   See O'Neill, "Beyond Trending."

7   Sarah Ahmed, *Differences That Matter: Feminist Theory and Postmodernism* (Cambridge: Cambridge University Press, 1998), 125.

8   Ibid.

9   John Roberts, "Collaboration as a problem of art's cultural form," *Third Text*, vol. 18, no. 6, 2004, 557–64, doi: 10.1080/0952882042000284961.

10 See Charlotte Barnes, "Marion von Osten on her collaborative style and multiple roles," *OnCurating*, issue 19 "On Artistic and Curatorial Authorship," June 2013, 89.

11 Rogoff, "Curating/Curatorial," 35.

12 Raqs in Eva Maddox, "We Will Follow in Your Afterglow," *Art Dose*, August 5, 2020, available at http://artdose. in/we-will-follow-in-your-afterglow/ (accessed October 8, 2020).

13 For an outline of this systemic interconnectedness, see, for instance, Benjamin Fallon, Dave Beech, Kirsteen Macdonald, and Marina Vishmidt, "Editorial introduction," *PARSE Journal*, # 9, on "Work,"

spring 2019, available at https://
parsejournal.com/journal/#work
(accessed April 1, 2023).

14 For the tension around "the curatorial"
and the "paracuratorial", see the
conversation between Jens Hoffmann
and Maria Lind, "To Show or Not
to Show", *Mousse*, no. 31, November
2011.

15 Tara McDowell, "The Post-
Occupational Condition," *Australian
and New Zealand Journal of
Art*, vol. 16, no. 1, 2016, 26 doi:
10.1080/14434318.2016.1171723.

16 Paul O'Neill, "Exhibitions as Curatorial
Constellations," in *Curating After the
Global: Roadmaps for the Present*,
ed. Paul O'Neill, Simon Sheikh, Lucy
Steeds, Mick Wilson (Cambridge, MA:
MIT Press, 2019), 436.

17 Ibid., 502.

18 Ibid.

19 See Isabelle Stengers, "Introductory
Notes to an Ecology of Practices,"
Cultural Studies Review, vol. 11, no. 1,
March 2005, 183–96. Alternatives
could possibly come from other areas
of post-humanist and new materialist
thinking, as proposed by Karen Barad
for instance. However, the ubiquitous
take-up of the term "entanglement,"
often without further specification and
qualification, potentially voids the
potential of this term too. I see scope
to combine Stengers's ideas with
some of Barad's, but that requires
a longer essay.

20 See Isabelle Stengers in Casper
Bruun Jensen and Line Marie
Thorsen, "Reclaiming Imagination:
Speculative SF as an Art of
Consequences. An Interview with
Isabelle Stengers," *NatureCulture*,
2018, available at https://www.
natcult.net/interviews/reclaiming-
imagination-speculative-sf-as-an-art-
of-consequences/ (accessed April 1
2023).

21 Although Stengers borrows her notion
of "ecology" from Donna Haraway,
it is worth underlining that her use is
less concerned with connotations
of "nature" than with its more generic
meaning of "environment."

22 Stengers, "Reclaiming Imagination."

23 Maria Lind, "Performing the
Curatorial. An Introduction," in
*Performing the Curatorial: Within and
Beyond Art*, ed. Maria Lind (Berlin:
Sternberg Press, 2012), 20.

24 Stengers, "Reclaiming Imagination."

25 See, for instance, Anton Vidokle,
"Art Without Artists," *e-flux Journal*,
16, May 2010, available at https://
www.e-flux.com/journal/16/61285/
art-without-artists/ (accessed April 1,
2023). Which is exactly where socially
engaged practices could be argued
to build bridges and break through
boundaries; my argument is that
despite the plurality of the vocabulary
at hand, to some extent it continues to
counter such understanding.

26 In her 2009 outline of "the curatorial,"
Lind also suggests that an expanded
notion of curating situates it as
"a multidimensional role that includes
critique, editing, education, and
fundraising," effectively highlighting
that the creative aspect that tends
to attract the limelight is only part
of a much more complex range of
tasks and roles under the position of
"curator."

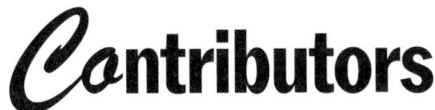

Contributors

María Berríos is a Chilean sociologist, writer, educator and curator. Her work explores issues traversing art, culture, and politics within Latin America. In particular, her work examines collective experiments of "Third World" alliances and their exhibition formats, such as the Solidarity Museum Salvador Allende (1971-to date) and the Havana Cultural Congress (1968). She has been a professor and a guest tutor in several universities and art academies in Europe and Latin America and has published her work extensively. She was one of four curators of the 11th Berlin Biennale (2019–2020) and is currently Director of Curatorial Programs and Research at MACBA (Barcelona).

Pip Day is a curator, writer, educator and advisor based in Berlin with a practice of long-term collaborative research, programming, mentorship and change-making within cultural institutions.

From 2012–2020 she served as Director/Curator at SBC Gallery
of Contemporary Art in Tiohtià:ke/Montréal. While based in Mexico
City, she founded el-instituto (2008-present) and was Director of
teratoma's city-wide Residencias Internacionales en México (RIM)
and Estudios Curatoriales, the first curatorial studies program in
Latin America. Pip has taught on curatorial MFA programs at Bard
College, the RCA and Goldsmiths.

Nikolett Erőss is a curator based in Budapest, Hungary. She is
a founding member of the curatorial team of OFF-Biennale Budapest,
and since 2018 she has worked for the Budapest History Museum's
Budapest Gallery, of which she has served as Department Head
since 2022. She holds a Master's Degree in art history from ELTE
Budapest. From 2003 and 2008 she was Editor of the online
contemporary art magazine: exindex.hu. From 2006 to 2010 she
was Curator at Trafó Gallery, later working at the Ludwig Museum -
Museum of Contemporary Art as Curator until 2013. From 2016–2018
she was Co-editor and Writer for mezosfera.org.

Elizabeth Larison is Director of the Arts & Culture Advocacy
Program at the National Coalition Against Censorship in New York,
leading initiatives advising artists, curators, and institutions in how
to address the presentation of controversial artworks. Previously,
Elizabeth served as Director of Operations, and before that,
Director of Public Programs at apexart, and has worked in curatorial
capacities for Flux Factory, the Park Avenue Armory, the Judd
Foundation, and the Vera List Center for Art and Politics. She holds
a MA in Curatorial Studies from Bard College.

Dr. Eszter Lázár is a curator and associate professor based in
Budapest. In addition to teaching in the Department of Art Theory &
Curatorial Studies at the Hungarian University of Fine Arts,
she curates exhibitions and collaborates on projects. She was
a member of the working group for the Curatorial Dictionary project
of tranzit.hu and in the Film Section of the international RomArchive
project. She joined the curatorial team of the OFF-Biennale Budapest
in 2019 and with the collective, she took part in documenta 15 in
2022. She is currently a senior researcher in an H2020 project on
artistic research as part of the EU4ART Alliance.

Nina Möntmann is Professor of Art Theory at the University of Cologne, PI at the Global South Study Center (GSSC) at the University of Cologne, as well as a curator and writer. Her publications include Decentring the Museum: Contemporary Art Institutions and Colonial Legacy, Kunst als Sozialer Raum and the edited volumes Brave New Work: A Reader on Harun Farocki's film 'A New Product,' Scandalous: A Reader on Art & Ethics, New Communities, and Art and Its Institutions. Recent exhibitions include Naeem Mohaiemen: Langer Tag at Temporary Gallery and Kölnischer Kunstverein, Cologne (2023), Magic Bureaucracy at Tensta konsthall, Stockholm (2017), and FLUIDITY at Kunstverein in Hamburg (co-curator, 2016).

Serubiri Moses is a Ugandan curator and author based in New York City. He currently serves as faculty in Art History at Hunter College, CUNY, and visiting faculty at the Center for Curatorial Studies, Bard College. He previously held teaching positions at New York University and the New Centre for Research and Practice (DE/US), Dark Study (US), and Digital Earth Fellowship (NL). As a curator, he has organized exhibitions at museums including MoMA PS1, Long Island City; Kunst-Werke Institute for Contemporary Art, Berlin; and the Hessel Museum, Bard College, NY. He serves on the editorial team of e-flux journal.

Dr. Bonaventure Soh Bejeng Ndikung is a curator, author, and biotechnologist. He is the Director and Chief Curator at Haus der Kulturen der Welt, Berlin. He was founder and Artistic Director of SAVVY Contemporary Berlin, 2009–2022; Artistic Director of Sonsbeek 20 to 24, Arnhem, 2020–2022; Artistic Director of 14th Rencontres de Bamako, Mali, 2022; Curator of the Finnish Pavilion, 58th Venice Biennale, 2019; Guest Curator of the Dakar Biennale of Contemporary African Art, 2018; and Curator-at-Large of documenta 14, Athens and Kassel, 2017.

Sofía Olascoaga works at the intersections of art and education by activating spaces for critical thinking and collective action. She was Co-curator of the 32nd Bienal de São Paulo Incerteza Viva; Academic Curator at MUAC (Museo Universitario de Arte Contemporáneo – UNAM) in Mexico City, 2014-15; Director of the education department at Museo de Arte Carrillo Gil, 2007–2010; Workshop Clinics Director at International Symposium of Contemporary Art Theory, 2012; Research Curatorial Fellow at Independent Curators International, 2011; and Helena Rubinstein Curatorial Fellow at the Whitney Museum of American Art's Independent Study Program, 2010.

Dr. Paul O'Neill is an Irish curator, artist, writer, and educator. He is the Artistic Director of PUBLICS, a curatorial agency with a dedicated library, event space, and reading room in Helsinki, Finland. Between 2013–17, he was Director of the Graduate Program at the Center for Curatorial Studies (CCS), Bard College. He was International Tutor on the de Appel Curatorial Program, Amsterdam; Curatorial Research Fellow with Situations, Bristol; and has held many lecturing and senior research positions since the mid-1990s, including in the MFA program in Curating, Goldsmiths, University of London, and Visual Culture, Middlesex University. He is author of The Culture of Curating and the Curating of Culture(s) (2012), translated into many languages, and (co-)edited numerous critical anthologies on curating. Most recently Paul has published three artist books as co-editor: Maryam Jafri: Independence Days (2022), Kathrin Bohm: Art on the Scale of Life (2023), and Dave McKenzie Banners and Letters (2023). Two new publications of his curatorial texts called CURIOUS and CURED are planned for publication in 2024.

Agnieszka Pindera is a curator based in Warsaw who worked at the Muzeum Sztuki in Łódź (2016-23) and Museum of the History of Polish Jews (2014-16). Previously she worked at the Centre of Contemporary Art (CoCA) in Toruń from 2008 to 2011. In 2013 Agnieszka was co-curator, with Daniel Muzyczuk, of Konrad Smoleński's exhibition Everything Was Forever, Until It Was No More in the Polish Pavilion at the 55th Venice Biennale.

Dr. Gregory Sholette is a New York-based artist, writer, teacher and activist. He is a Professor at Queens College, City University of New York (CUNY),and a Co-Director of Social Practice CUNY headquartered in the Center for the Humanities, Graduate Center. Sholette holds a PhD in History and Memory Studies from the University of Amsterdam, The Netherlands, and is a graduate of the Whitney Independent Study Program in Critical Theory. His most recent book is *The Art of Activism and the Activism of Art* (2021).

The Teen Advisory Boards working within **PRAKSIS** (Oslo) and **Index** (Stockholm) are youth-driven leadership groups which participate in and advise the activities of each respective arts organization. These Teen Advisory Boards are open to creative people and organizers between 16–21 years old, and offer members the opportunity to develop experiences, and establish knowledge and networks within the cultural industry. The programs aim to inspire, strengthen and engage their participants to create their own space within the field.

Dr. Gerrie van Noord is an educator and curator of publications, based in London. She has worked on a wide range of publishing projects, including the Afterlives series for Artangel and Fabrications for Book Works. Recent projects include a selection of artist Isabel Nolan's writing, a website on Olivia Plender's work, and she was co-editor of a book on Kathrin's Böhm's practice, titled *Art on the Scale of Life* (2023). With Paul O'Neill, and others, she has worked on several critical anthologies on curating. Gerrie has taught at the MFA at the Glasgow School of Art, at Birkbeck, University of London, and currently she is a lecturer on the MA Curating Contemporary Art program at the Royal College of Art, London.